# Prevent Life Decay

- ...a compelling revolt against disease, depression, aging and toxicity
- ....unveils the mysteries of healing with fasting firepower, while it persuasively escorts the reader to a mountain moving life

## Marvin Yakos Ph.D.

xulon
PRESS

# Disclaimer

*"Where there's no counsel the people fall, but in the multitude of counselors there's safety."*
*(Proverbs 11:14)*

This book is intended for information purposes only and not to take the place of sound medical advice, to diagnose any ailment or to prescribe remedies. Anyone considering a fast of considerable duration, or herbal therapy, should consult a competent and duly appointed natural physician.

# Dedication

This book is dedicated to my wife Karen, and my children, Joshua, David, Amanda, Angela, and Jacob. You are the joy of my life.

# Contents

# Part 1
# Fasting Essentials

✦

# Lack of Knowledge

*"My people are destroyed for lack of knowledge." (Hosea 4:6)*

Why do we so often lead defeated lives? Why are we anxious, sluggish, overweight, unduly weak or lack self-control? Why do we fall prey to sickness and disease? Why are so many elderly on medication or lead poor quality lives? Why do statistics tell us we're getting progressively worse? How many of us search daily for healing in potions, lotions and pills for some shred of hope for a better tomorrow? How many of us are misled by profiteers? How many of us spend our health chasing wealth, and our wealth trying to buy back health? Why do we continue to buy the lies? Most of us take little notice of our innermost condition, until it's too late.

How many of us are aware of the stupefying amounts of chemicals that have been dumped on the withered American plains to make them fertile again? 1.2 billion pounds of poison are sprayed on American cropland every year. *(G.T. Sterling, "Health Effects of phenoxy herbicides" Scandinavian Journal of Work Environment Health 1986)* Our water and air are no less toxic. Some poisons, like DDT, take thousands of years to break down. As a result, sickness, disease and depression are rampant.

Are you a biological time bomb? Almost everyone has chemicals lodged in their bodies, especially in the fatty tissues. Animals, birds, and fish too are not immune. Cancer, obesity, diabetes, strokes and heart problems kill millions before their time. One in three Americans will get cancer, and we're supposed to be an advanced culture? We're being literally robbed of the nutrition it takes to fuel our bodies properly and sold ineffectual replacements. Profiteers are having a field day, misleading us, selling us addictive and useless garbage while they get rich on our ignorance.

> *"Very few people know what real health is, because*
> *most are occupied with killing themselves slowly."*
> —*Albert Szent-Gyorgyi, Ph.D. Nobel Prize*

What do we do? Where do we find the knowledge and wisdom necessary to overcome such silent and lethal adversaries? How do we obtain toxic relief? Do we really have access to the power of healing, rejuvenation and principles of longevity? Few people are aware of a simple and effective method to overcome such evils. The straightforward answers you'll find in this book may surprise you, challenge you and quite possibly change your life!

> *"What sculpture is to a block of marble, education is*
> *to the soul"* Addison

The foremost scientific and spiritual key to freedom from such corruption is fasting, but fasting has been out of vogue for thousands of years. The idea seems foreign, almost alien in today's overindulgent society. But wisdom from across the globe, both ancient and contemporary, suggests that fasting is a regular part of an advanced lifestyle, and as effective to our well-being as happiness, freedom and love. As we shall soon discover, not only is fasting a glorious and divine endowment, scientifically verified and historically supported, but a bona fide elixir of life and the very key to rejuvenation and health.

The central principle of fasting is the voluntary denial of the otherwise normal function of eating food for the purpose of individual growth. We fast to destroy seeds of deterioration in our lives and to overcome those malevolent influences that can't be defeated any other way. We fast in response to spiritual instruction, for discipline, cleansing, detoxification, and weight loss. We fast to examine and humble ourselves. We fast to seek after truth and to draw near to a God so precious, thereby giving Him our undivided attention. Fasting is a most powerful discipline, whereby divine power can be released in our lives! I pray fasting will enable the reader to experience deep cleansing in a fresh way, and experience all the wonderful healing and rejuvenating benefits that follow.

# Civilizations and Great Personalities that Fasted

*"Be ye doers of the word, not hearers only, thereby deceiving your own selves." (James 1:22)*

Fasting is known and practiced the world over, in great cultures, as well as in remote, little known lands. In Indonesia, the Javanese define an irreligious person as: *"One who does not believe in God, who never fasts, and who has no order in life."* Tribes with little or no modern contact practice fasting. In many primitive societies there's a strong belief that fasting frees the spirit for higher revelation. Certain tribes use fasting to initiate youngsters into adulthood. From generation to generation, for thousands of years, people across our planet have fasted.

Every religion on earth encourages fasting. Religious creeds mentioned fasting time and again. When we take a close look at historical icons, be they spiritual, artistic, political or highly intellectual, we find a most curious common thread among them. Most fasted, unlocking doors to creativity and vision, and then accomplished the exemplary! And what's even more striking, is the fact that they shared this universal truth across the span of thousands of years.

John the Baptist fasted and taught his disciples to do so. Jesus fasted for forty days for strength and to connect with the will of the Father before He began His earthly ministry. *"And Jesus being full of the Holy Spirit returned from Jordan, and was led by the Spirit into the wilderness, being forty days tempted of the devil. And in those days he did eat nothing; and when they were ended, he afterward hungered."* *(Luke 4:1, 2)* If Jesus found fasting important, perhaps it's significant. Jesus expected his disciples to fast too, but He didn't leave any hard and fast rules, other than refraining from hypocrisy. Fasting is left up to the individual, private and purely voluntary.

Buddhists fast to find the middle way. Moslems fast every day from sunrise to sunset the entire month of Ramadan. Jews observe four prescribed fast days a year as an expression of oneness with God. Moses asked the Jews to fast on the Day of Atonement. In the Talmud an entire volume is dedicated to fasting and Jewish theology contains many other books that refer to fasting. Jews practice a total fast, twenty-six hours with no food or water. They may not even brush their teeth or take a bath.

> *"When I went up into the mountain to receive the tablets of stone, the tablets of the covenant which the Lord made with you, then I stayed on the mountain forty days and forty nights. I neither ate bread, nor drank water."* *(Deuteronomy 9:9)*

The prophet Daniel fasted as he prepared to receive revelations concerning the latter days. It was when Daniel distinctly understood that the desolation of seventy years was coming to an end, that he *"...set his face to seek unto the Lord God by prayer and supplications with fasting"* *(cf. Dan. 9:3).* Hannah fasted when she desired God to give her a son. Anna fasted in the temple while she served God. Isaiah, Nehemiah, Zechariah, Shadrach, Meshach, and Abed-Nego fasted for spiritual strength. Elijah fasted in order to learn which prophet would succeed him, and for help in discerning the next king. The entire Jewish population in Persia fasted to save their land in time of great crisis. At the time, the situation was critical, as Haman, like Hitler, had conspired to kill every Jew in the land.

Leaders of many nations fasted throughout history for their country. The founding fathers of America fasted.

> *"If My people, which are called by My name, shall humble themselves, and pray, and seek My face, and turn from their wicked ways; then will I hear from heaven, and will forgive their sin, and will heal their land"* *(2 Chronicles 7:14)*

Several Old Testament personalities such as Jehoshaphat, Joel, Esther, and Ezra, called for group fasts in time of great need. David fasted a week for a child's illness. He also fasted as he wrote some of the Psalms.

> *"...I humbled myself with fasting"* *(Psalm 35:13)*
> *"... I wept, and chastened my soul with fasting"* *(Psalm 69:10)*

David also fasted to mourn Abner. *(2 Samuel 3:35)* Why did these biblical personalities fast? Is there a common thread? Is fasting somehow connected to uncommon achievement? A general answer is found in *(Matthew 23:12)* *"And whoever exalts himself will be abased, and whoever humbles himself will be exalted"*

In the book of Acts, Cornelius wanted spiritual answers and fasted. He met an angel who told him where he could find Peter. Saul fasted three days after he was knocked off his donkey and blinded on the road to Damascus. After God renamed him Paul, he also fasted fourteen days and heard from an angel with manifold revelations. It's recorded that Paul fasted with Barnabas before they made important administrative decisions and before they left for missionary journeys. Luke, the physician, who wrote one of the four gospels, fasted twice a week.

We find great personalities fasted in the secular world also. Hippocrates, the father of modern medicine, lived four hundred years before Jesus. He lived to the ripe old age of ninety and fasted often. He not only recommended fasting for everyone, but also encouraged its prolonged use.

The early Christian church prescribed four designated fast days. They encouraged fasting on a regular basis in order to retain spiritual purity. Diverse Christian leaders, revivalists and men and women of renown fasted, such as Martin Luther, Rees Howells, John Wesley, Teresa of Avila, Joan of Arc, David Brainard, Jonathan Edwards, John Calvin, George Muller, Charles Finney, and John Knox. Catherine of Sienna went into ecstatic trances and wouldn't eat for weeks. Francis of Assisi did 40-day epiphany fasts every year prior to the season of Lent.

The Essenes, (meaning expectant of one who is to come or healer), authored the Dead Sea Scrolls and fasted regularly to enhance communion with God. Many Essenes are said to have lived to be more than one hundred and twenty years old. King Henry the VIII instituted public fasting, as had Romans, and other nations in times of fear or war. Fasting brought focus and people together. Puritans fasted, as did Pilgrims to find direction from God before they set sail for the New World in the Mayflower.

Fasting is not relegated to the groups or personalities we've mentioned, but it's a universal principle of life that can work for anyone. Diverse peoples from almost every culture and era in history have fasted to purify the spirit, to cleanse and renew the body and to sharpen the intellect. Even a newborn baby naturally refuses food when ill.

In the dictionary fasting is most often defined as voluntary abstinence from food. For our intents and purposes we shall use the following definition: *"Fasting allows our beings, at their deepest levels, to turn from biological stimulation and nourishment, to a direct and deep divine absorption to its most beneficial end, spiritual, mental, and physical."*

The great Indian pacifist, Gandhi, to save the soul of India, fasted while he walked fifteen hundred miles from New Delhi to the seaport of Bombay. He fasted in defiance of the British salt policies. Gandhi so inspired his countrymen that Indians eventually drove the British out of India using his principle of ahimsa, or nonviolence. Gandhi requested his followers to fast in order to purify themselves, and to find peace and joy on earth. Gandhi said: *"Fasting will bring spiritual rebirth to those who fast and purify their bodies........... The light of the world will illuminate you when you fast and purify yourself."* The tiny, dhoti (common cloth) clad ascetic often fasted a week or two in order to show his love and communicate deeply with his fellow man. What he could not accomplish with words he did with fasting.

Ayurveda, India's ancient holistic remedial science, recommends every healthy person fast one day a week. It closely coincides with the Biblical teaching, *"...Physician, heal thyself." (Luke 4:23)* The Chinese philosopher Confucius fasted, as did great artists and inventors like Leonardo da Vinci, Galen, and Michael Angelo. Andre Shakarov, the renowned Russian physicist, fasted. American Indians and their medicine men fasted prior to going into forests and mountains in search of healing herbs. Indians claimed fasting gave them a clearer vision as to which herbs and medicines would help heal their tribal infirmities. The Indians also fasted before various rituals and in sweat lodges for spiritual guidance.

Great thinkers have been responsible for giving our culture philosophy, logic and reason, and many of the basic intellectual platforms that have become the very basis for Western thought. The personalities who developed these platforms fasted, people like Socrates, Plato, Epicteus, Zarathrustra and Plotinus.

Plutarch, the famous Greek biographer said: *"Instead of medicine, fast a day."*

Plato practiced ten-day fasts for clarity before he wrote dissertations. The 40-day fast was also practiced by Plato, as well as by Aristotle. Pythagoras, who founded modern geometry, actually required his disciples to fast 40 days before he initiated them into the mysteries of his teachings. Pythagoras felt that only by fasting could his students go deep enough to perceive the profound truths of life. Regardless of their diverse teachings, all these thinkers agreed they could better perceive reality when they fasted. Aesculapius, a famous doctor of ancient Greece advised his fellow countrymen; *"Instead of using medicine, fast."* Paracelsus, the great medieval physician said; *"Fasting is the greatest remedy."*

Different civilizations used fasting to cure disease and sickness.

Egyptians fasted in an effort to cure syphilis. More recently, in 1882, Dr. Isaac Jennings, a renowned naturopathic doctor, brought therapeutic fasting to the forefront of modern consciousness in an effort to help people heal themselves. Fasting, as handed down to us by these great personalities, has remained a part of many civilizations but has gained only moderate acceptance in modern times. These personalities discovered the power of fasting, practiced it, and through fasting, found the focus and intensity it takes to open areas they may have never accessed. Not only had the great personalities of old discovered the secrets of fasting, but also today, in clinics worldwide, scientists and medical professionals are documenting its multitude of benefits. These findings have been backed up with scientific studies and mountains of clinical data. As a result, a well-informed and knowledgeable segment of the naturalist medical community no longer smirks at fasting.

Aside from all the physical, intellectual, and mental benefits, fasting was effectively practiced for forgiveness, for protection and divine intervention, for direction, to combat spiritual enemies, for self control, for spiritual breakthroughs, for empowerment, and overall communion with God.

Over two thousand years ago, the Essenes wrote about the basics of healing: *"........the word and power of God will not enter into you, because all manner of abominations have their dwelling in your body and your spirit; for the body is the temple of the spirit, and the spirit is the temple of God. Purify, therefore, the temple that is worthy of Him... Renew yourselves and fast. For I tell you truly that Satan and his plagues may only be cast out by fasting and prayer (See also Mark 9:29). Go by yourself and fast alone...... The living God shall see it and great will be your reward. And fast till Beelzebub and all his evil spirits depart from you, and all the angels of our earthly Mother come and see you (harmony with nature). For I tell you truly, except you fast, you shall never be free from the power of Satan's diseases. Fast and pray fervently, and seeking the power of the living God for your healing."*

# Beyond Medicine

Fasting is the most effective and oldest healing method known to mankind. It's simple, and best of all, free! Nature loudly demonstrates that fasting is good medicine, as we automatically lose our appetites when sick. Even a cat or dog knows that it should fast when there's a problem. Animals instinctually fast when ill, lying down in a restful location until better. Almost anyone can fast and discover the deep, time-proven methods that lead to rejuvenation and healing. Researchers have now clinically proven that impurities are burned up in the body during a fast, which clears the mind, rests our inner organs, and creates the most favorable inner climate for healing. Sickness may simply reflect an overloaded immune system—one burdened by exposure to toxic substances of various kinds. By fasting only one day a week, almost anyone can eliminate these toxins and rebuild their immune system to help fight off infectious illnesses and degenerative diseases. Fasting can even help slow the aging process.

The merits of fasting depicted in this book are not meant to hinder or replace responsible medical wisdom or one's walk with God, but in effect, to become a vital part of it. You may ask, what's all this fleshy stuff? Oh how we forget that the focus of most great spiritual leaders, as well as the ministry of Christ, was to the whole person. We find as far back as Leviticus 21:16-23 that physical health was actually mandatory for spiritual leaders before they were allowed to minister. Evil will manifest physically, emotionally and mentally, as well as spiritually, and Jesus with miracle after miracle destroyed it on every level. Jesus touched all need, all suffering with the tender hands of a divine healer. *"...For this purpose the Son of God was manifested, that he might destroy the works of the devil: (I John 3:8)*

While a God seeker fasts primarily for spiritual purposes, we shouldn't be overly surprised that God recommends a practice that also helps the mind and body. God wants His children to be healthy and happy, and to have an abundant life.

> *"Dear Friend, I wish above all things that you may prosper and be in health even as the soul prospers."* (3 John 2)

Obeying spiritual principles produces blessings. A person need not only fast, as we shall discover, because it's the best therapeutic practice known to mankind, but so much more so because our spiritual hunger is deep, our need to intercede is acute and spiritual warfare is increasingly intense. Most of all, God teaches us that fasting is important! An appropriate fast will facilitate divine freedom, fulfillment and restoration!

The Bible describes the fast God chose for us in *(Isaiah 58:6-11)* *"Is this not the fast that I have chosen: To loose the bonds of wickedness, to undo the heavy burdens, to let the oppressed go free, and that you break every yoke? Is it not to share your bread with the hungry and that you bring to your house the poor who are cast out; when you see the naked, that you cover him, and not hide yourself from your own flesh? Then your light shall break forth like the morning, your healing shall spring forth speedily, and your righteousness shall go before you; the glory of the Lord shall be your rear guard. Then you shall call and the Lord will answer. You shall cry and He will say, "Here I am." If you take away the yoke from our midst, the pointing of the finger, and speaking wickedness, if you extend your soul to the hungry and satisfy the afflicted soul, then your light shall dawn in the darkness, and your darkness shall be as the noonday. The Lord will guide you continually, and satisfy your soul in drought, and strengthen your bones; you shall be like a watered garden, and like a spring of water, whose waters do not fail."*

Fasting, along with prayer, is a most effective way to develop spiritual muscle. Fasting draws us into a deep inner struggle where we need God's grace the most. We shouldn't fast primarily to earn something; but we can take fasting to its ultimate conclusion, and that's to make a connection with God. By fasting we can clean out the pipeline that connects us to the anointing of God. Our spiritual fabric becomes corroded through the normal course of living in a polluted world, and the best way to cleanse is through prayer and fasting.

At the deepest level, fasting connects us to God and prepares us to receive spiritual authority. *"And I will give unto thee the keys of the kingdom of heaven..." (Matthew 16:19) "Fear not, little flock; for it is your Father's good pleasure to give you the kingdom." (Luke 12:32)* Along with prayer, praise, worship, and intercession, fasting is one of the most powerful keys to growth and overall prosperity God offers. Unfortunately, in today's world of excess and spiritual ignorance, this key is obscure and nearly lost. As we shall soon discover, during a fast we can shed things we couldn't reach or remove any other way. Along with physical impurities, emotional weaknesses can be exposed and brought to the surface for elimination. At the highest level, fasting can be a statement saying God is more important than anything else. Fasting isn't a magic formula, but it helps to develop the state of being required by God's promises. Fasting isn't a cure, but the process that facilitates the cure. It's a "divine endowment" to an overburdened mind, body and soul. It's extremely effective in creating an internal environment where the body can do what it does best —heal itself. Fasting with God in the equation will move you to your potential, your birthright, increase your happiness, and bring you to your optimal health.

Hippocrates, the father of modern medicine stated, *"A wise man should consider that health is the greatest human blessing."*

It can take years to break a body down. It can take time to build it up. But with proper knowledge and wisdom, it can be done. Does all this sound too simple? Scriptures inform us that spiritual principles are made simple to confound the wise. (I Corinthians 1:27) The assertion is that spiritual principles are simple so even a child can understand them. For our intents and purposes, there's no need for complex formulas, sensationalism or exaggerated aggrandizement, but only straightforward scientific, experiential, and spiritual principles. We'll explore the scientific to the supernatural, shining a bright light on the simple principles that lead to healing, restoration and levels not ordinarily accessed!

# Is Fasting Safe?

*"Where there is no counsel, the people fall; but in a
multitude of counselors there is safety."*
*(Proverbs 11:14)*

**P**eople that most commonly criticize fasting usually know the
least about it, and that includes much of today's mainstream
medical establishment. Psychologists have called it anti-social, irrational and bizarre. Other common reactions are apprehension, fear,
laughter, ignorance, derision, and excuses. Fasting is curiously
suspect in the eyes of the profiteers. Some people actually think
fasting is starvation. But we find that the word *starve* comes from
German root *sterben*, which means *to die*, whereas fasting comes
from *fest*, a word meaning *steadfast* or *standing firm*.

Jesus instructed his disciples that fasting and prayer were tools
to increase faith to its highest dimension. He proposed the combination of prayer and fasting as powerful supernatural tools designed to
remove overwhelmingly malicious influences from the human
condition. This supernatural potential can't be measured by doctors
or scientists, but on a purely physical level, there are splendid
results recorded in the annals of natural science. We'll hear testimonies, explore spiritual principles, consider experience, and
examine these databases of medical science. We'll also go behind
the scenes of world famous fasting clinics to hear what the doctors

who run them say about fasting.

Drs. J. Kellberg and P. Reizenstein of the world-renowned Karolinska Institute in Stockholm, which awards the Nobel Prize in Medicine each year, clinically monitored in-hospital patients in fasting studies lasting up to 55 days, demonstrating that scientific, prolonged fasting is not only perfectly safe for most, but also therapeutically beneficial as well. There are hundreds of fasting clinics and centers throughout Europe, where therapeutic juice-fasting has long been used as the premier weight-loss, detoxification and healing modality.

German and Swedish biological clinics, operated by medical doctors, routinely treat virtually every disease, from cardiovascular and digestive disorders to rheumatic and skin conditions with scientific, therapeutic fasting. In Russia, fasting has been used for a half-century as the most effective treatment for schizophrenia, with irrefutable studies showing that 70% of patients improved mentally after 20-to-30 days of controlled fasting. Similarly, one Japanese research clinic fasted 382 patients, all suffering psychosomatic disease, with a success rate of 87%.

Dr. Charles Goodrich of the Mt. Sinai School of Medicine in New York City said, *"People don't realize that the chief obstacle to fasting is overcoming the cultural, social and psychological fears of going without food. These fears are ingrained. . . .However, fasting is not starving, not even in a medical sense or the natural sense."* Dr. George Cahill of Harvard Medical School emphasized the point: *"Man's survival [of long abstentions from food] is predicated upon a remarkable ability to conserve the relatively limited body protein stores, while utilizing fat as the primary energy producing food."*

The general clinical definition of fasting is to abstain from food. The spiritual definition is to abstain from food and to hold fast to something supernatural. Whatever the definition or reason for a fast, a person stops ingesting, swallowing, digesting, chewing, metabolizing, storing, and eliminating food. When a person fasts, the body in its natural wisdom alters its metabolic rate and focuses on rejuvenation, healing and restoration. It's this agenda that's disputed by some and lauded by others. We'll find much of what happens during a fast can be easily explained.

There have been hundreds of thousands of supervised fasts that have been documented worldwide. As the information age rapidly shrinks our world, this data is being compiled with more accuracy, in greater amounts, and with more frequency than ever. There are over 500 medical journal articles available on therapeutic fasting that have summarily concluded that fasting results are based on permanent biological laws. Natural hygienic practitioners and doctors have monitored and supervised fasts, some up to forty days on water alone, and juice fasts of over two hundred days. Extraordinary and uncommon fasts have been recorded. A man fasted for 74 days in the forest without food on a suicide attempt and ended up feeling so rejuvenated he returned to civilization and lived another 30 years. One woman fasted for 249 days on juice alone! Another man fasted 143 days! Doctors have proven that a person can live without food for many months, but the same person could kill himself or herself by overeating in just a few weeks.

The human body is designed to naturally rid itself of poison, to heal itself if only given the opportunity. It's been alleged that there can be 5 to 10 pounds of toxic chemicals locked in the average adult's cell tissue and organ storage areas. With such alarming and overburdening statistics coming to light, it's not a question of if fasting is safe, but that not fasting is unsafe!

> *"Every patient carries her or his own doctor inside."*
> —*Albert Schweitzer*

> *"Everyone has a doctor in him or her; we just have to help it in its work. The natural healing force within each one of us is the greatest force in getting well. Our food should be our medicine. Our medicine should be our food. But to eat when you are sick is to feed your sickness."* Hippocrates, M.D

Surviving without nourishment seems to defy human experience. Because of this, people are misinformed and fearful of fasting. Such irrational fear is closely related to lack of self-control prevalent in our society, and related to the deluge of food excess and other bad habits that debilitate us all. In America, many more people suffer from overeating and intoxication than they do from malnutrition. Often the mere mention of fasting brings forth a negative response, defense mechanisms, and ignorant rationalizations that originate in the subtle regions of food addictions. We're a nation addicted to excess. Nowhere is this more evident than in our eating habits.

As with any subject like fasting, where humans struggle to understand profound truths, there are differing schools of thought. Polarized experts like Dr. Bragg (water fasting) and Dr. Airola (juice fasting), not only consider fasting safe, but exuberantly encourage its use for almost everyone. Major fasting clinics, with cumulative data from over 150,000 supervised fasts, consider fasting totally safe. The Buchinger clinic in Germany, which has supervised approximately 90,000 fasts, claims fasting is the fastest and safest recovery and healing process known to man. Author and naturopath, Dr. Airola, claims that a person can go 100 days on a supervised juice fast with absolutely no danger. Hundreds of thousands of people have successfully fasted in clinics throughout Europe, where fasting seems to be more accepted and even popular. In Europe 14-21 day fasts are commonplace and considered completely safe and therapeutic for almost anyone.

Scientifically speaking, and given adequate fluid intake, the body is able to maintain the fasting state as long as fat stores and other non essential materials exist, a period of approximately 10-15 weeks in a well-nourished adult. However, once the fat reserves are exhausted, starvation begins and there's a rapid loss of protein as the body invades the structural components of cells for needed fuel. Once the starvation process begins, it progresses quickly to death as proteins needed for critical activities of cells are degraded and the ability of the body to maintain itself is compromised.

Dr. Airola, in his book, *Juice Fasting* writes: *"The Karolinska Institute in Stockholm, the world-famous medical research institution, has made clinical studies and experiments with fasting under the direction of Drs. P. Reizenstein and J. Kellberg. Supervised fasts' lasting up to 55 days showed that fasting is not only safe, but that it also has definite beneficial therapeutic properties."*

It's been proven time and time again that fasting doesn't damage the body, but quite the contrary, fasting is a time-honored tradition that provides us with a multitude of benefits, many of which, could not be obtained any other way. One of humanity's greatest discoveries is our God-given innate ability to cleanse, rejuvenate, regenerate and truly heal ourselves.

Comedian Dick Gregory lost nearly 200 lbs. from his obese frame and kept it off for over 30 years. Then he ran from Los Angeles to Chicago, averaging nearly two marathons a day for 40 straight days, while juice-fasting. People often have the notion that a normal, healthy person will get weak and depleted during a fast. Quite the contrary, they'll find unexpected energy, health and rejuvenation. Dr. Buchinger calls fasting *"A Royal Road to Healing"*.

*"All the participants in the famous Swedish Fast Marches of both 1954 and 1964, led by Dr. Lennart Edren, walked 325 miles over 10 days—from Gothenburg to Stockholm—with no solid food at all. And, as participant Karl-Otto Aly, M.D., concluded, "The marches clearly showed that humans can live for an extended period without food, and even accomplish a hard, physical effort while fasting. The general, expressed feeling among participants was that they felt stronger and had more vigor and vitality after the fast, than before it!"* Dr. Ragnar Berg, a nutritional expert and winner of the Nobel Prize, labeled the fasting experiments in Sweden as *"great scientific successes"*.

In December 1903, eight athletes entered an athletic contest in Madison Square Garden. Amazingly, all were on the 7th day of a water fast. Joseph H. Waltering, one of the eight, won both the 50-yard dash and the 220-yard run. Another member of the eight, Gilman Low, won first prize in the strength contests. The following day, on the eighth day of his fast, in front of 16,000 well-fed spectators munching on popcorn and peanuts, he established nine world records for strength and endurance that would stand for years.

Nonetheless, fasting should not be misused. Fasting is a private and significant personal decision. A person should understand what they're doing before they ever begin. (*See Chapter on People That Shouldn't Fast*) When an aspiring faster becomes sufficiently educated, they'll realize fasting is perfectly safe, and they'll find an elixir of life spiritually, mentally, and physically. When I first realized fasting actually worked and personally started to experience the benefits, I could barely contain my excitement.

From the Buchinger Clinic in Germany: *"We must restore fasting to the place it occupied in an ancient hierarchy of values "above medicine". We must rediscover it and restore it to honor because it is a necessity. A beneficial fast of several weeks, as practiced in the earliest days of the Church, was to give strength, life, and health to the body and soul of all Christians who had the courage to practice it."*

If fasting is considered safe by the Father of Western Medicine, Hippocrates, it's probably safe for you, as well. After all, Jesus fasted. Would Jesus do harmful things and encourage others to do it?

*"Let he who has ears to hear, let him hear!" Matthew (11:15)*

# Length, Place, and Best Time for a Fast

➣<

*"To everything there is a season, a time for every purpose under heaven." (Ecclesiastes 3:1)*

John's disciples came to Jesus and asked him why they fasted while Jesus' disciples did not. Jesus answered; *"Can the friends of the bridegroom mourn as long as the bridegroom is with them? But the days will come, when the bridegroom shall be taken from them, and then shall they fast."* (*Matthew 9:15*)

The Bible makes no specific mention of the best time, length, or the best place to fast. There are many examples of fasts of different lengths, from partial fasts of giving up certain kinds of foods for a time, to an eighty-day fast with no food or water. Daniel fasted 21 days. Esther and Mordecai fasted 3 days and nights. Jesus fasted 40 days in the wilderness. But frequently the Bible makes no mention of how long people fasted. For example, it's never mentioned how long Ezra fasted before making his journey to Jerusalem (*Ezra 8:21-23*).

Length, time, and place are a matter of choice. Times for a fast can be when we're tempted, when wisdom is earnestly desired, when help and protection are needed, for victory over powerful demonic powers, in mourning, for impossible situations, when prayer is not answered, for new ministries, during intense spiritual battle, and for repentance and revival. (*Mat. 4:2, 17:21 Dan. 9:3 Ezra 8:21-23; 2 Chronicles. 20:3 Jeremiah. 36:9 Mk. 9:29 Est. 4:10-17; 9:31 Nehemiah. 1:4, 9:1-2 1 Sam. 1:6-7 2 Sam. 1:12 Acts 13:2-3; 14:23 2 Cor. 6:5, 11:27 Joel 1:14; 2:12; 2:15*)

There are no scriptures which command fasting at a specific time or for a specific occasion, but a fast was usually for one day (*Judges 20:26; 1 Samuel 14:24; 2 Samuel 1:12; 3:35*) from sunrise to sunset, and then after sundown food would be taken. However, some fasts were longer. The length of time you fast should be determined by choice or divine leading. A person may decide to fast whenever there's a spiritual concern or major struggle in their life. There may be times when we participate in a group fast, as was done by Saul in (1 Samuel 14:24) or Jehoshaphat in (2 Chronicles 20:3). But ultimately that decision is solely between God and us.

Shorter fasts are easier to endure until a person builds "spiritual muscle." A three-day fast is beneficial for spiritual or physical cleansing. Paul the apostle fasted upon conversion, and after three days of cleansing, received the Holy Spirit and his eyesight returned (*Acts 9:17-18*). Three-day fasts are also especially helpful in breaking addictions.

Depending on whether the fast is for spiritual reasons or merely a physical cleansing, the length, place, and time may vary. Unless God has "unmistakably" led you, the level of experience of the faster should be considered carefully. Each person has a different genetic makeup, metabolism, diet, health, and toxicity. After a person does a few short fasts, they can familiarize themselves with the reactions they experience and slowly build on experience. Wisdom should be employed, and desire too, plays a prominent role, as it's difficult to teach or encourage a person to do anything they don't want to do. *"You've got to have the want to"*

One's environment should be conducive to a fast and peaceful, with the least amount of stress possible. A natural setting is best and fasting is easier in a warm climate. If a person wants to fast during winter or in colder climates, they should take necessary precautions to stay warm. During a deep, spiritual fast, a person should find a quiet place without worldly interruptions. Jesus went to the desert, an inhumane but quiet place where he could be alone with the Father.

A heavy physical work schedule should be reduced, or alleviated altogether to allow for optimum rest and healing. The age of the person is also important. The amount of toxins in a person's system should be carefully noted. Common sense and wisdom must prevail, and ample counsel taken before undertaking a fast of any considerable duration. Regardless of these particular considerations, fasting is recommended and should be undertaken as soon as possible.

Dr. Shelton, a fasting expert said: *"The time to fast is when it is needed. I am of the decided opinion that delays pay no dividends; that, due to the fact that the progressive development of pathological changes in the structures of the body with the consequent impairment of its functions does not cease until its cause has been completely or thoroughly removed. Putting off the time for a fast only invites added trouble and makes a longer fast necessary, if indeed; it does not make the fast futile. I do not believe that any condition of impaired health should be tolerated and permitted to become greater. Now is the time to begin the work of restoring health; not next week, next summer, or next year."*

Jesus and the prophet Moses fasted for forty days and forty nights. Moses fasted forty days and nights before he went up Mt. Sinai to obtain the Ten Commandments, and fasted another forty days and nights when he came down without food and water, a scientific impossibility. This was an absolute fast and was the greatest fast ever recorded. Moses' fast was undoubtedly a supernatural fast, because he not only refrained from food, but from water as well. No one can fast eighty days without water without divine intervention. Does that mean we should follow Jesus, Moses, and the prophets and rush headlong into such a lengthy fast? Definitely not! Sufficient wisdom should be used so that the fast is done safely and with lasting benefit.

A short, devotional fast of one day can be done by almost anyone at anytime with little or no experience. If a person undergoes spring-cleaning, a cleansing fast of seven to ten days is recommended by most experts and should be sufficient. But such a fast should be done only after one has practiced shorter one to three day fasts. Short fasts are most effective when done regularly on a schedule, like one day a week. If a person isn't consistent, a short fast will produce short results.

A healing or deep therapeutic fast can range from seven to over forty days, and can be done with either water or juice. Any lengthy fast over ten days must definitely be approached with proper knowledge, and for ultimate safety and benefit, should be supervised by a knowledgeable health practitioner until sufficient experience is gained.

For most people, a three-day fast is an excellent introduction to fasting. This short fast has adequate benefits and can be practiced by virtually anyone at anytime, anywhere. Three-day fasts can be undertaken for spiritual benefit, to lose weight, for cleansing, to break bad habits, change diets, or to rest the organs of the body. As the first one to three days are the most difficult, it's sometimes a shame to stop there. If you start on a three-day fast and feel good, you may choose to continue the fast.

A seven to fourteen day fast should also be normal and safe for just about anyone, but again, anyone that is new to fasting should have supervision if fasting for any considerable length. The supervisor should be a veteran faster, bestowing confidence, security, and a positive attitude. A full medical checkup should be undertaken by anyone considering a long fast, especially if the fast is intended for health reasons.

Dr. Bragg, who supervised fasts for over sixty years, considered a ten-day fast safe and more than adequate for most physical reasons. Most clinical and supervised fasting proponents still consider a twenty-day fast or less, short. A fast less than twenty days should not be difficult, as hunger pains usually disappear altogether after about three days.

When a person begins a fast the body instinctually understands its duties are redirected to cleansing and healing. After the first few days, the person should actually begin to feel more focused and develop a sense of well-being. Some people experience euphoria, which is sometimes due to the fact that they have never cleaned or rejuvenated their body, or they've always had an overly stuffed colon. Some people, once they clean out a modest amount of toxins, have exclaimed that they feel better than ever.

If a novice decides on a long fast of over twenty-one days, it should definitely be supervised. They also need to be very sensitive and aware of the time when hunger returns. The time to break the fast should be obvious, as the hunger will be accompanied by an "on-going" desire to chew, an attraction to the aroma of food, and an innate desire for protein. If a person doesn't break a fast when real hunger sets in, the body will begin the starvation process and consume itself. This, however, will not occur for quite a long time.

The longest fast on record is a juice fast of 365 days, one entire year! Dr. Allan Cott, in *The Ultimate Diet*, states that no person should starve before 28 days of fasting. This, of course, takes into account that a person doesn't have a serious illness or severe health problems. Starvation starts when the body begins to feed upon itself and consume essential tissues, organs, and muscle. Essential elements of our bodies are those we need to sustain life. If a person's schedule becomes too heavy during a long fast and they're overly stressed, they should break the fast.

Experience is a good teacher. The more often a person fasts, the longer they'll be able to fast and the more toxins the body will expel. It may have taken years to accumulate poisons, sometimes a lifetime. It may take a long time to expel them all. A 21-day fast is rather short when you consider a person who has developed bad habits and ingested toxins over an entire lifetime. One short fast won't necessarily clear up a poisoned body or set the stage for healing a chronic problem. It's highly recommend that a toxic person initially do a number of short fasts, perhaps several one day fasts, then graduate to several three day fasts before attempting a longer fast. In this way the body will gradually eliminate poisons and not flush them all into the system at once and overburden the lymph system. A very long fast may be necessary to repair a chronic condition, in which case great care is needed in planning. If the fast is to be done for chronic healing purposes, a person needs to arrange a quiet restful place where there's minimal stress and few distractions. With patience a person can learn as they go along and come to understand their own body and level of health.

Anyone can begin at anytime. As a recap; a person new to fasting should fast one day, then graduate to a three day fast. Gradually, as the novice faster gains experience and insights into their body and toxicity levels, they can increase to longer periods. Regulation, consistency, a good diet, and good habits are necessary in between fasts. The body has its own healing power, and when given the proper conditions, it will heal. A combination of good habits is better than a one-time long fast a person thinks will cure all their ills. If a person maintains a regular fasting program, the results will accumulate in due time. *Keep in mind that any lengthy fast should be under consultation of a bona fide expert.

*"But let patience have its perfect work, that you may be perfect and complete, lacking nothing."*

*(James 1:4)*

# Detoxification and Preparing for a Fast

*"Nine out of ten men are suicides" Ben Franklin*

**W**hy should anyone alter their lifestyle and go through the trouble to detoxify? There's more than one reason, and sadly, detoxification is quite necessary for good health in our day and age. Over the last few decades, mankind has drastically altered the chemistry in our environment. Hundreds of millions of pounds of chemicals have been released into the ground, threatening our soil, ground water, lakes and rivers. A billion pounds of chemical emissions have been released into the air we breathe. In 1996 alone, 2,433,506,582 pounds of chemicals were released into the environment we live in.

> *"Do not be deceived, God is not mocked, for what-ever a man sows, that he will also reap."*
> *(Galatians 6:7)*

To multiply the problem, we've refined away much of the nutritional value of our food and replaced it with artificial colorings, indigestible chemicals, preservatives, and profit enhancers. Then we add antibiotics and other foreign chemicals to our systems to combat these ills. Toxicity occurs when such harmful materials overcome the beneficial bacteria in the intestinal tract. The unhealthy bacteria also release toxic by-products into our circulation, the combination of which can severely impact our health. Eventually the body's inability to rid itself of this onslaught of poisons results in disease and the loss of quality of life.

It's highly impractical to think anyone can avoid toxicity. Regardless of how diligent we can be, toxicity will continue to threaten our quality of life and severely impact our health. So what can be done? We need to take responsibility for our health and that involves learning how to protect our bodies. We can sanitize our immediate environment of chemicals, dyes, paints, solvents, glues, acids, insecticides, harmful cleaning agents and remove them if possible. In some cities, an air cleaner may be necessary. We should eat fresh, wholesome foods and avoid refined foods, refined sugars, additives and preservatives. It's important to drink clean water and plenty of it. Due to the terrible assault from our polluted environment, it's most important to support our body's natural efforts and its ability to eliminate toxicity.

One practical solution is to nourish the body's natural detoxification mechanism with nutrients required to attain the best possible detoxification activity. High quality natural foods and water or juices are best. Zinc and pathothenic acid, L-glutamine, and acidophilus provide support for the intestines. In a proper state of health, the intestines promote elimination of toxins through regular bowel movements. This keeps toxins from spilling over into our blood stream and into other vital organs. Vitamins A, B3. B6, C, and E, beta-carotene, the amino acids L-cysteine and L-glutamine, glutathione and phospholipids support liver function. In a healthy system, the liver filters out and transforms toxic substances in the blood into harmless substances that can be excreted in the urine. Vitamins A, C, B6, magnesium and potassium support optimum kidney function. Fat provides storage for toxins and should be minimized.

Is detoxification too high a price to pay for health? Would a person forego the benefits because of a little discomfort? When a person refuses to detoxify and fast for lack of effort, they've chosen to block the most powerful prevention and healing principles available to them short of divine healing or a miracle. When we're sick we may need to take medicine, which can be bitter. Once we take bitter medicine, we eventually get better, and then things become sweet. Conversely, things that make us sick are usually sweet and easy in the beginning, such as eating too much food, illicit sex, drinking alcohol, or taking drugs. But what happens to the illusion of sweet as time goes on? It turns bitter. When a person drinks alcohol, it can be fun, but then it all turns so bitter. The next morning there's a hangover, and if the habit persists, the bitter consequences are well known.

> *"Who has woe? Who has sorrow? Who has contentions? Who has complaints? Who has wounds without cause? Those who linger long at wine. Those who go in search of mixed wine. Do not look upon the wine when it is red, when it sparkles in the cup, when it swirls around smoothly. At the last it bites like a serpent and stings like a viper." (Proverbs 23:29-32)*

A person can become intoxicated and experience many a sweet high from many different allurements, but if it's not healthy or natural, it'll eventually turn bitter, even deadly. Too much food can lead to overburdening our systems and obesity. Alcohol can ruin the liver and mind. Drugs have a multitude of ill effects. They all wreak havoc on the heart and brain. Fasting may seem bitter at times, but the results will be very, very sweet.

When preparing for a fast, determination is most important. A person must have the want to. Medicinal remedies, detoxification, spiritual formulas, herbs, diet, and fasting may have no lasting effect if there's a bad attitude.

> *"It is much more important to know what sort of a person has a disease than what sort of disease a person has." Sir Wm. Osler*

There's a deluge of anger, hate, envy and fear in the minds and emotions of mankind, so detoxification is also necessary for the byproducts created by these unbearable attitudes. These woes are fostered by TV, movies, music, relationships, as well as the stress caused by everyday life. Unforgiveness and repressed anger can get stored throughout the human organism, eventually causing serious disorders. When anger is continually suppressed, a toxicosis develops in the brain consisting of the overproduction of neurotransmitters that processes the anger, and hormone balance is disrupted. Just like deadly poison, this accumulation is the source of a long list of future chronic maladies, like depression, addictions, bipolar disorder, low self-esteem, compulsive behavior, intense mood swings, nervous disorders, including Parkinson's and Alzheimer's disease, social violence and crime. We hear interpretations of these subtle diseases daily, cloaked in remedial terms like low-blood sugar, candida albicans, and chronic fatigue syndrome. Most of these maladies are simply the result of physical, emotional or mental toxicity and can be easily overcome through detoxification, fasting and a change of habits.

> *"A person will get well when he is tired of being sick." Loa Tsu*

Toxicosis, or poisoning, generally occurs when negative electrical charges increase in the brain. Neurons periodically eject too much or too little of the neurotransmitter molecules and periodic anxiety and depression occur. Depression is also caused by the clogging of receptors with neuro-chemicals and with substances from the environment such as unmetabolized food substances, chemicals and other toxins. When physical, emotional and mental toxicity combine, it causes untold pain and suffering. We're offered medication to simply cover up the ills so we don't feel them, and the downward spiral continues until there's a major disease. If we don't detoxify and clean out the debris on all levels we'll age faster and lose our quality of life as we go.

When toxic cells die they're usually replaced by new cells, however toxic neurons generally aren't replaced. They break open and release toxins during what can be called a detoxification crisis of intense anxiety or other symptoms. Without getting too technical, these events trigger a sort of domino effect on the nervous system, organs and brain. The excess electrical activity overexcites the nervous system causing excitatory nervous symptoms that range from mild anxiety to mania and even to extreme acts of violence. Anger repressed becomes rage when it escapes, or if never allowed to vent, extreme depression. Scripture warns of repressing anger. *"Be angry and sin not. Don't let the sun go down on your wrath" (Ephesians 4:26)* If people would only detoxify and fast, a good percentage of the mental illness in our society would simply disappear.

Recovery from alcohol involves the release of the toxic accumulations in the body. Neural pathways need to be cleared for normal neurotransmission to be restored. Once these toxins are cleared, there's the likelihood that anxiety, depression, mental disorders and addictions will also disappear.

A nervous breakdown is the body's natural response in breaking of neurons to release toxins. Tears and tantrums are natural detoxifiers for our emotions. Often when a person repents of depraved behavior, the repentance is accompanied by intense weeping, as the emotions release guilt and shame and the body is freed from the chemistry of sin. Edgar Allen Poe in *"The Tell-Tale Heart"* wrote that insanity is nothing more than an overactive nervous system. On a purely physiological level, he intuitively understood that his character was driven mad by the loud beating of his own heart, an activity associated with fear and anger and accelerated by the release of toxic neuro-chemicals. Of course, once we rid our systems of toxicity we must then learn to practice habits and principles that keep them from reoccurring. Today's variety of therapies and psychoanalysis flail with futility at the stored poisoned lurking in our spirits, minds, bodies and emotions.

When the process of detoxification removes poisonous elements from our beings, beneficial changes begin to rapidly occur. Blood pressure, temperature, and pulse normalize. Palpitations disappear. Glucose and cholesterol levels decrease. Hypothyroidism disappears. Colds and other minor disorders minimize. Digestion is stronger. People get relief from constipation, headaches, allergies, backaches, colitis, peptic ulcer, dizziness, addictions, menstrual cramps, skin disorders, stomach pains, nausea and teeth grinding. They fall asleep easily and sleep restfully.

One of the most harmful effects of toxicosis in the brain is the inability of the body to carry out the daily process of detoxification and elimination as it was naturally meant to. Since the sympathetic nervous system increases cellular metabolism, it accelerates the release of toxins throughout the body. Because of toxicosis in the brain, this system is periodically over and under-excited. This means that detoxification events, which might be expressed as a cold or other acute disease, will be periodic and intense. When sympathetic nervous system activity is suppressed, toxins will accumulate throughout the body. Tumors can occur anywhere in the body where toxins are being walled-off, and they are likely to contribute to cancer.

Proper nutrition will help prevent deficiencies and toxicosis. There are many helpful dietary changes that help to reduce, prevent and alleviate damaging toxic buildups in our systems. Green tea, wheat or barley grass juices are laced with vitamins, minerals and antioxidants. Fresh organic fruits and vegetables juices are nutritious and help remove toxins. Try to avoid produce that has been sprayed with pesticides and harmful fertilizers.

Here are a just few nutritional aids. Coenzyme Q-10 is an antioxidant that carries oxygen to the tissues and strengthens the immune system. Q-10 is also a key to a healthy heart and metabolic balance. Copper assists the body in eliminating toxins, while folic acid strengthens immunity. Magnesium used with calcium helps reduce stress, while vitamin B aids in improving general health, helps relieve stress, and aids liver function. Vitamins C, E and zinc taken with copper are also good antioxidants. Vitamin C is also required for the absorption of other vitamins and minerals. Herbs such as Acacia catechu fight free radicals, which have been proven to be cancer causing. Dandelion root supports the blood and liver, is a diuretic, treats liver damage and is a mild laxative. Garlic is a great antibiotic, antimicrobial, antioxidant, inhibits infection and strengthens the immune system.

Gingko biloba neutralizes free radicals that are often produced during stress. Goldenseal helps detoxification and strengthens immunity. Hawthorn Berries increases circulation, especially to the brain and extremities, and are another source of Vitamin C. Milk thistle is an antioxidant, helping in blood and liver detoxification and in neutralizing free radicals. Turmeric aids liver function. Uncaria fights free radicals. *(Portions of the preceding material in this Chapter taken from The Toxic Mind: The Biology of Mental Illness and Violence)*

There are far too many reasons to detoxify, and fortunately there are many ways we can help the process along, none better than fasting. Once we've determined to fast, a slow buildup is recommended. A person can prepare for a fast with elimination and detox diets that can be helpful to begin the discharge of indigestible and waste products from the body. It's important not to splurge with food before a fast with the attitude, I'm going to fast anyway, so why not splurge. Such an attitude will only lead the body to initially work on the excess foods that were ingested, and the person will forego some of the benefits of the fast.

Detoxification has clear objectives. It'll revitalize tissues and cells, and clean and strengthen the organs, blood and brain. When we don't detoxify and eliminate waste, we cause autointoxication, or self-poisoning. There are many detoxification regimens, mostly based on watery diets, such as herbal broth, lemon drinks, grape drinks, herbal teas, and cider vinegar. They all have similar results. Most bitter tasting herbs are detoxifying and have alkaline properties that neutralize harmful acids in the system. Hot baths are also recommended during this period, and enemas can be used for the first few days. When beginning detoxification, a comprehensive program is necessary, such as a proper diet of fresh food, plenty of water, exercise, elimination of stress, good bowel movements and proper rest.

A person intent on a fast should wind down their food intake and modify their diet, perhaps eating more raw fruits, juices, salads and vegetables. This can be done for two or three days preceding a fast. Common sense tells us that as a person approaches the first fast day, they should consume less solid food.

Natural purgatives can be helpful. There are plenty of natural laxatives that will suffice. Herbs such as ginger and sage induce perspiration, and in turn help throw off toxins. Licorice root is a mild laxative, though not good for people with high blood pressure. Cayenne is a blood purifier. Psyllium seeds are colon cleansers and help induce elimination. When combined with water, psyllium seeds absorb ten to fifteen times their weight in water. Flaxseed and chia seeds are also non-irritating laxatives. Clay of bentonite also eliminates poisons. (See Chapter on Colon for more detail)

Such preparation may be necessary because our body may hold too many toxins and chemicals in the tissues. We're exposed to pesticides, inorganic fertilizers, herbicides, prescription drugs, preservatives, additives of all kinds, and chemicals from our air, food and water. Poison is used on the farm, in our homes, offices and in the car. A person on a healthy diet with no bad habits will generally not be as toxic as a person addicted to unwholesome food, alcohol, drugs, or cigarettes, but there's no escape.

In our contemporary polluted cultures, one short or mid-range fast will not detoxify a person, but the greatest result will come from many fasts. The more one fasts the more progress is made. Bad habits will be broken and replaced with strong, healthy habits. Also, as a person gains experience, with each succeeding fast, they become better at it. A person should accumulate as much knowledge as possible before entering a fast.

Until we learn to stop the dreadful dumping of petroleum products, industrial waste, and other chemicals into nature, we'll continue to be at risk. Hoards of people walk about with untold symptoms and diseases caused by such toxins. These unnatural elements are hard on our bodies and cleansing organs. When the body is overburdened, we feel tired, stressed and depressed. When we're loaded with toxins we often get headaches, which act like a signal or an alarm clock in the brain letting us know that something is wrong. Since the brain is made up of 60% fat, and toxins accumulate in fat, headaches are the natural result. Rather than clean out the cause, our culture simply covers this symptom with an aspirin or heavier drugs. Eruptions of the skin can signal internal problems and toxic overload, as can weakness, sluggishness, allergies, irregular breathing, high or low blood pressure, bodily temperature changes and digestive and elimination problems. It's a vicious cycle. Toxins create disease and disease creates toxins. Detoxification eliminates these toxins and makes the body strong enough to fight against them.

We can buy herbal detoxification products or concoct our own, as different herbs affect different organs. Depending on our individual situations and constitutions, we can modify a detoxification program to help alleviate the unwanted stress on our bodies. Toxins may be somewhat neutralized with hot, pungent herbs such as ginger and hot peppers. These herbs help to stimulate the digestion fire, which will begin to feed on impurities as one begins a fast. (See Chapter on Herbs)

Herbs are to be used in moderation and in conjunction with good habits and knowledge. (*See Chapter on Herbs*) Overuse and continued use of certain herbs can lead to resistance by our bodies, so by selective use and by alternating herbs, the body will remain responsive. Detoxification helps set up a fast, but the best detoxification known to mankind, is the fast itself.

# Fasting and Rejuvenation

*"Or do you not know that your body is the temple of the Holy Spirit who is in you?" (I Corinthians 6:19)*

For years I struggled to rejuvenate, longing for peak energy. I didn't like feeling tired or sluggish. But everything I tried came to a fruitless end, and promises of the so-called present day health philosophies came up empty. As I got older being in great health got even harder, especially staying fit. Then I stumbled onto the ancient principles of fasting after reading a book by Dr. Paul Bragg, and soon discovered the miracle of fasting.

There are people living genuine spiritual lives with deep, heartfelt commitments to God. Some have found peace in the deepest spiritual sense. Shouldn't they also enjoy physical prosperity and bountiful energy? In our true state, the body can be a temple for God's Spirit. Would we fill such a temple with refuse and poison? If our temple were out of shape, overweight, and dirty, would we not clean it? Given the opportunity, would we not put this bodily temple into the best shape we can?

Dr. Paul Bragg was well ahead of his time. He's credited with starting the first health food store in California. Though he'd been ridiculed for his fasting programs, nonetheless, thousands of people were influenced by his example. Their testimonies of healing and rejuvenation are his vindication. Dr. Bragg overcame a severe illness by fasting and became a testimony himself.

When he was a great grandfather and highly respected in the natural health field, he once challenged the salt theory. He believed the use of salt to be unnecessary. He challenged ten athletes from a Southern California university to a competition. He proposed that he and the strong young athletes walk from Furnace Creek Ranch to Stovepipe Wells in Death Valley, a distance of some thirty miles. Death Valley, located in the Mojave Desert is the lowest and hottest place in the US. The challenge was simple. Walk across. There would be a few minor differences between the athletes and Dr. Bragg. The athletes would take water and salt tablets. They would also be followed by a station wagon full of food. Dr. Bragg wouldn't eat, but fast the entire way and drink only warm water.

*"Great peace have those that love your law, and nothing causes them to stumble." (Psalms 119:165)*

The desert air was a sizzling 105 degrees the morning they began. The young men were lively, eating sandwiches, drinking soda, and joking about the old man. The sun blazed and grew hotter as they walked, and one by one, the young men wilted in the oppressive heat. At noon the temperature climbed to 130 degrees. Some of the young men vomited their saturated bowels into the desert. Others complained of various pains. Some got dizzy, while yet others became violently ill. None of them made it across. They were driven back to the ranch in the station wagon. Only Dr. Bragg made it across! The next morning, just to prove his point, he continued his fast and walked back, another 30 miles, smiling, and joking about the young men. Until Dr. Bragg passed away at the age of 96 in an unfortunate swimming accident, he remained full of vim and vigor, enjoying God's abundant life. He's a wonderful example of the profound benefits of fasting.

For centuries explorers sought the Fountain of Youth. Researchers continue to seek ways to arrest aging. Youthing spas have sprung up across the globe. Regardless, many elderly are feeble and senile by the time they reach their later years. God promised mankind just before the flood that their life spans would no longer exceed one hundred and twenty years, but also said that those years could be full and healthy.

Not only should we expect long lives, but to live in fullness and health. All we need is proper knowledge. We need to apply the proper formula. We no longer need to be destroyed for lack of knowledge. The quotes in this book aren't frivolous promises made up by wishful dreamers, but the voice of experience, scientific documentation, spiritual principles and age-old tradition. The promises of longevity that come from scripture will work, but only when the proper knowledge is applied, and only when people are obedient, and doers of the word.

> *"My son, do not forget my law, but let your heart keep my commands; for length of days and long life and peace the will add to you." (Proverbs 3:1-2)*

Dr. Bragg said; *"The greatest discovery by modern man is the power to rejuvenate himself physically, mentally, and spiritually with rational fasting."* Dr. Bragg simply discovered and acted upon an age-old principle written into scripture thousands of years ago.

Dr. Bragg, and many like him, never participated in or accepted the deterioration that sets in by following ways of profit, greed, and overindulgence. He stayed away from over-processed foods and intoxication. He detoxified his organs often, and fasted to stay healthy and young. He understood what happens on the cellular level when we don't heed natural laws. When there's a breakdown of the tissues and organs at the cellular level it causes whole scale deterioration, degeneration and rapid aging. We don't have to accept the debilitating results of our present day environment and lifestyles. There are answers and ample knowledge available to counteract the poison about us.

> *"Hear, my son, and receive the words of my sayings, and the years of your life will be many."*
> *(Proverbs 4:10)*

Most people have the potential for a healthy 100-year life span.

There are 32,000 people that are a hundred years old in the US alone. The Spanish explorer Ponce de Leon searched the Americas for the fountain of youth, but we've a fountain of youth within us. We can activate it by fasting! It's a clinically proven fact that fasting rejuvenates and makes a person look and feel younger. In a study where mice fasted every three days, their life span increased by 40%!

Arnold Ehret, one of the West's foremost proponents of rational fasting for physical, mental and spiritual rejuvenation, termed fasting the *"Master Key"* to mental and spiritual enfoldment and evolution, especially during these degenerate times. He said, *"Fasting's spiritual benefits are its greatest gift, those which make life truly worth living. All human hearts are welcome here, whatever their color, creed, condition or philosophy, because everyone is just like you and me, wanting happiness and disliking suffering. In other words, seeking joy and freedom from suffering is the birthright of all beings."*

The body rejuvenates itself automatically during a fast. Due to the absence of food the body has extra energy, since it doesn't have to digest, assimilate, and eliminate. The body instinctually redirects this energy to revitalize every cell in our bodies. Taste buds, hearing, smell, touch, and eyesight improve. Auras burn brighter. Vigor increases. We lose weight and feel more youthful. Blood pressure is reduced. Hearts are strengthened. Sexual energy is increased. Acne is reduced and the skin is smoother. Blotches disappear and our eyes are whiter. Every part of our bodies is revitalized. Fasting gives our bodies the facility to clean, rebuild and recharge. The curative force throws off toxins, clears dead cells and balances our delicate chemistry.

Even our tiniest links need to be strengthened. Billions of these cells are being replaced daily. Though miniscule, cells are like tiny sponges that absorb what we breathe, eat, drink and apply to the skin. Cell degeneration is primarily caused by waste materials and toxins. About one quarter of our cells are either dying, very old or need to be replaced. Unless our body gets rid of the diseased and dying cells it can't build new ones. Every cell undergoes rejuvenation when we do a serious fast. Foreign substances and dead cells are removed. Revitalized cells resist debilitation and disease, and allow the rest of the body to run more efficiently.

Hans Selye, the famous Canadian Stress Doctor, says, *"Life, the biological chain that holds our parts together, is only as strong as the weakest vital link".*

As we've noted, during the fasting process digestive enzymes are relieved of duties and help cleanse and revitalize the body, but fasting also stimulates the building of new cells. Aging occurs when we have more dead cells than live cells. Conversely, youthing, as some call it, occurs when we have more live cells than dead cells. After a fast, one of the first things a person notices is a more youthful appearance. Fasting rejuvenates a person physically, mentally and spiritually. Hippocrates, the father of modern medicine said; *"Everyone has a doctor in him, we just need to help him in his work."* Do you really want to change your life? You really can! Start today.

*Dr. Paul Bragg states; "Fasting clears away the little things which clutter the heart and mind. It cuts through the corrosion, renewing our contact with God."*

# People That Shouldn't Fast

There's a time to fast, and people that need to fast. But there are also people that shouldn't fast and a time to refrain from fasting. Most determinations are common sense. If a person has too much stress they should resolve the greater part of the problem before fasting. Those that do heavy, physical labor shouldn't fast very long. When strength and stamina are noticeably reduced, a person shouldn't fast. A pregnant woman shouldn't fast, as she's responsible for the nourishment of her child, as are nursing mothers (as detoxification could poison their baby). A Hypoglycemic can fast, but needs to be careful. Severely emaciated people and diabetics on insulin need sound medical advice. Fasting is discouraged for people with Tuberculosis and Graves disease. Each case is unique and should be considered separately.

If a person suffers from advanced cancer, diabetes, heart disease, tuberculosis, cardiovascular disorder, kidney or liver diseases, or neurological degenerative disorders, they should be under direct medical supervision. Fasting is inadvisable for children not yet fully grown (still forming bone and teeth) and those suffering from wasting disease. A person shouldn't fast in cases of tissue loss or severe physical trauma.

If a person has been diagnosed as terminal, a fast could exorcise the faith necessary to move the mountain, but the person could also die sooner. Such a person should consult a physician and other counselors, and above all, pray for guidance. Fasting under such conditions means either taking your life into your own hands or placing it into the will of God. I think that when a person is terminal, such a decision is a very personal matter. I would trust God and fast. God would either take me or I'd be healed. I would trust God's word and his process. There's little to lose when terminally ill, and there has been more than one case where people have fasted and been totally cured.

People on long-term or heavy medication shouldn't fast. Most drugs will produce more harmful side effects than normal when not combined with food. Drug therapy often just masks the symptoms anyway and causes severe side effects. If heavy drugs are discontinued, there may be withdrawals, thus a person shouldn't fast right away and seek special consultation. Most allopathic doctors have little experience or knowledge concerning fasting or natural healing, so a reputable holistic doctor should be sought.

If a person is doing herbal therapy, the dosage should be cut down to a third, as the body will use herbs more efficiently and will respond more promptly during a fast. A person that's seriously underweight should also be careful, though it has been proven that fasting can promote healing and chemical balance, and weight may eventually be normalized. Again, consultation is necessary.

Anorexics that stop eating while entertaining a distorted image of who they are, shouldn't fast, but seek counseling and healing for their spiritual and mental disorders. Bulimics, who binge only to forcefully vomit, and then repeat the process, should also seek consultation and get to the root of their problems before they fast. Expert advice can be found at a bona fide fasting clinic that has experience in such matters, ample clinical data and competent physicians.

For most others, fasting is perfectly safe and even recommended. For thousands of years fasting has been lauded for healing diseases, as well as helping people retrieve healthy dispositions. Expert doctors claim that juice fasting can be undertaken at home without any supervision. Though unpleasant symptoms may accompany a fast, this is usually normal as the body is throwing off unwanted debris. Everyone is different. There are many factors that determine whether or not a person can fast for a long period of time, but generally, fasting is considered suitable for everyone by great spiritual and scientific minds alike.

> *"Fasting does no harm, and is always worth trying."*
> *Dr. Otto Buchinger*

# Benefits of a Fast

*"The head is clearer, the health is better, the heart is lighter, and the purse is heavier." Scottish clergyman*

Fasting is a powerful and effective means to promote health, longevity and vibrant life, and overcoming the hindrances of fatigue, toxicity, obesity and illness. Fasting focuses on our insides, and when the insides are taken care of, the outside will be fine. Fasting can cleanse and restore a person on every level. People that fast feel lighter, energized, and notice marked improvements in complexion and eye color. It's a scientific fact that by fasting a person will heal faster, and may extend their life several years.

Dr. Herbert Shelton, the world-renowned hygienist said: *"Fasting is the best way to maintain good health, eliminate pain and disease, reduce, and control weight."* Dr. Shelton also stated: *"The freedom and ease you experience during abstinence enables you to discover new, undreamed of depths of meaning of life"*.

In *Fasting and Eating for Health*, Joel Fuhrman, M.D., notes, p. 10: *"The fast does not merely detoxify; it also breaks down superfluous tissue—fat, abnormal cells, athermanous plaque, and tumors, and releases diseased tissues and their cellular products into the circulation for elimination. Toxic or unwanted materials circulate in our bloodstream and lymphatic tissues, and are deposited in and released from our fat stores and other tissues. An important element of fasting detoxification is mobilizing the toxins from their storage areas. This process occurs best and most efficiently during total fasting."*

Invisible toxins, chemicals, metals and parasites settle in our bodies and can cause chronic pain and disease. Frequently, people as well as their doctors can be unaware of the root cause of the symptoms they experience. People often travel from doctor to doctor and never find the root cause. As an example, a clogged, putrefied colon can cause depression. Fasting has been said to be like wringing out a sponge full of dirty water. By cleaning out the body, fasting can help heal and prevent dozens of these diseases.

*When health is absent, wisdom cannot reveal itself; art cannot become manifest; strength cannot be exerted, and reason is powerless." Ardmore Herophilus M.D., 300 B.C., Father of Anatomy and physician to Alexander the Great*

Dr. Buchinger also stated, *"Fasting is, without any doubt, the most effective biological method of treatment. It is the operation without surgery. It is a cure involving exudation, reattunement, redirection, loosening up and purified relaxation. While fasting, the patient improves her or his physical health and gains much. But he or she will have neglected the most important thing if the hunger for spiritual nourishment that manifests itself during fasting is not satisfied."*

### Need An Overhaul?

1. Fasting cures disorders and relieves the body of all types of poisons and toxins
2. Helps a body heal faster and is preventative
3. Builds resistance to disease and resists infection
4. Rejuvenates our bodies down to the cellular level
5. Extends life
6. Burns unnecessary fat
7. Builds physical stamina
8. Rests our vital organs while it destroys sick and superfluous substances
9. Helps develop muscular flexibility

10. Improves intestinal and stomach passages and strengthens connective tissue
11. Restores gall bladder function
12. Restores our ability to assimilate nutrients
13. Lessens the fat content in the blood
14. Regulates sediment and blood sugar in the blood
15. Reduces high blood pressure
16. Cleanses and thins the blood
17. Strengthens our nerves
18. Helps us to look and feel younger
19. Clears the complexion
20. Cleanses our joints
21. Sharpens our minds
22. Makes us more alert
23. Releases tension
24. Helps us sleep less
25. Allows for an easy and free exchange of gases
26. Strengthens the heart
27. Diminishes deposits in the arteries
28. Destroys fat in the vascular walls
29. Gives us a feeling of greater self-assurance
30. Provides an enhanced capacity for prayer
31. Increases our immunity
32. Overall, it leaves a person in the best possible shape
33. And most importantly, puts us in touch with God's infinite power and His abundant principles

People that fast, almost to the person, remark that their minds become clearer. This can be attributed to several reasons, but one of the main factors is that toxins are cleared from the blood, which helps relieve undue pressure on the brain. Not only does fasting relieve pressure on the brain, but the brain is intimately connected to every other part of the body, and when the other parts of the body are strengthened the brain again benefits.

Mountains of objectionable material can be removed during a well-employed fast. Deeply embedded loathsome material can be destroyed that might not be accessed any other way. Fasting can also be of significant help for degenerative diseases. Hope pours in from clinics worldwide as chronic illnesses, mysterious health problems and common diseases are diminished or completely cured by fasting. These are not absurd health claims made by some fanatic or sensationalist, but clinically observed and documented cases supported by increasing amounts of data.

### Some Conditions helped or completely eliminated by fasting

| | | |
|---|---|---|
| Arthritis | Neuritis | Emphysema |
| Obesity | Aging | Wrinkles |
| Bad Complexion | Dry skin | Back pain |
| Migraines | Psoriasis | Irregular heart beat |
| Asthma | Impotency | Chronic Bronchitis |
| Tonsillitis | Acne | High Blood Pressure |
| Kidney trouble | Measles | Colitis |
| Toxemia | Pimples | Blotches |
| Gout | Liver Trouble | Allergies |
| Skin Diseases | Hay Fever | Hives |
| Rheumatism | Insomnia | Inflammations |
| Ulcers | Boils | Low Blood Pressure |
| Digestive Disorder | Constipation | Tumors |
| Gum Disease | Bad Circulation | Stomach Complaints |
| Kidney Stones | Cancer | |

Common colds, the flu, and similar nagging illnesses are virtually eliminated when a person fasts and returns to healthy living. Such illnesses are simply the result of natural body functions that act like release valves. The body does what it has to do in order to unload unnecessary material and eliminate blockages that threaten it. When a person suffers from a common cold, cells release infection-fighting histamine, which produces a runny nose, watery eyes, and at times a sneeze to help unload unwanted debris. These are signs that the body needs balance and detoxification. This is a great time to fast, as a fast will resolve the problem faster. Mucous should not be dried or eliminated with modern day medicines. Mucous is simply the body's way of removing unwanted debris.

If a person is relatively healthy, the greatest physical benefit of fasting is prevention. A healthy faster can take vitality to a new level. One of the goals of fasting for prevention is to purify the body on the cellular level, to its deepest possible degree. This is a significant fast and a person may not have enough reserve to accomplish complete cellular cleaning all at one time. A person may have to fast many times to achieve this purpose. But results can be astounding! At the stage of cellular purity, a person should be as physically fit as possible. Signs that accompany a healthy body are a tremendous feeling of well- being, strong energy levels, a clear tongue, clear eyes, clear urine, and good body odor. Other healthy signs are pink color under the fingernails, a normal pulse rate, normal temperature, normal blood pressure, good muscle tone, clean skin and fresh breath.

> *"You don't have to sit passively by while your God-given entitlement is stolen right out from under you nose. There is toxic relief!" Don Colbert, M.D.*

Fasting can put an end to obesity, toxemia, sickness and mental confusion. It can reintroduce self-control into one's life and bring one to a spiritual, mental and physical depth never before experienced. Fasting can be the beginning of something new and fresh, and bring a person to the threshold of abundant life.

# What Happens During a Fast?

*"Privation of food at first brings a sensation of hunger, occasionally some nervous stimulation, but fasting also mobilizes certain hidden phenomena which are most important. The sugar of the liver and the fat of the subcutaneous deposits are mobilized, as are the proteins of the muscles and glands. All the organs sacrifice their own substances in order to maintain the blood, heart, and brain in a normal condition. Fasting purifies and profoundly modifies our tissues."*

*Dr. Alexis Carrel, Noble Prize winner*

Most of us take great pleasure in breaking bread at family outings, savoring sumptuous feasts, sneaking snacks at midnight and going back for seconds at all you can eat restaurants. So why would anyone want to be subjected to gnawing hunger pangs? We've read about the benefits of fasting, but what actually happens within the body when we deprive ourselves of nutrition? After all, food isn't only one of our most enjoyable activities, but necessary for life.

When we don't eat, our insides begin a symphonic chain reaction, as stomach walls contract in rhythmic fashion to let us know we need food. These hunger pains last approximately 30 seconds to 3 minutes and can reoccur on an average of every 12 1/2 minutes. When we don't fulfill this demand for food, the pain will last and even increase for a day or two, or even three. Somewhere between two to four days into a fast, hunger pains will weaken and then disappear altogether. Fasting shuts down the brain's appestat mechanism 3-to-4 days into the fast, precluding hunger pains from arising thereafter.

Fasting is giving up food for a specified period of time for a higher purpose, whether spiritual, mental or purely physical. Regardless of purpose, fasting takes effort and focus. As the faster gives up food, vision, clarity, direction or a healing is received in return. It should be noted that fasting itself does not heal. Power to heal and self-correct is already inherent in the body. But fasting does provide the optimum environment for healing, a perfect atmosphere to release that "certain hidden phenomenon of natural power" that not only removes the harshest of oppressions, but as a by product, helps to repair the body.

Within the body, there's constant interaction between health and disease. *Dis* means "deprived of" and *ease* means "comfort". As in spiritual struggles between good and evil, war is constantly waged in the body between disease fighting agents and disease causing agents. Fasting intensifies the battle and gives the edge to good. The body is healthy when balanced, when the fire of digestion is working at optimum strength, and when waste products are produced and excreted at normal levels. When there is dysfunction and imbalance, fasting is the safest and most efficient way to correct it.

> *"Life, the biological chain that holds our parts together, is only as strong as the weakest vital link."*
> *Hans Seyle*

Everyone is unique with different imbalances and toxic accumulations, and a different level of vitality in their organs. Everyone won't experience the same sensations or the same results during the fast. As each person's bodily system undergoes change, one can expect a gamut of reactions, from feelings of burning and stress to feelings of exhilaration and well-being. Some people feel an awareness of increased lightness with extreme clarity, while others flushing substantial amounts of toxins may be deluged with headaches and nausea.

The first fast a person undergoes may cause weakness in the early stages. During a fast, the body burns up and excretes large amounts of accumulated wastes. Drinking huge amounts of liquids helps facilitate this process. Sadly, many stop fasting at the first sign of tension with a false impression; unsuccessful to break through to the other side and encounter the joy and energy fasting affords. Fasting is like a knife that cuts away superficiality, cutting to the bone, and in the process removing what does not belong. When there is serious pollution in the body, this may hurt for a bit.

The following materials are usually eliminated during a fast: dead, dying or diseased cells, unwanted fatty tissue, trans-fatty acids, hardened coating of mucus on the intestinal walls, toxic or chemical waste matter in the lymphatic system and bloodstream, toxins in the spleen, liver, and kidneys, mucus from the lungs and sinuses, imbedded toxins in the cellular fibers and deeper organ tissues, deposits in the microscopic tubes responsible for nourishing brain cells, and excess cholesterol. However the greatest benefit of detoxifying the body is allowing the mind to function more efficiently, as well. In Plato's words; *"I fast for greater physical and mental efficiency."*

Not only are we cleansed of poisons during a fast, our tissues and the various glands renovated, but we rest digestive and assimilative organs. There's heightened clarity of consciousness resulting from the rejuvenating, regenerating and stabilizing effect on all the most vital physiological functions. Fasting restores and normalizes glandular, metabolic and nervous-system functions. It also speeds up the elimination of morbid accumulations, toxic wastes and dead cells, accelerates new cell and tissue generation and enhances cell-oxygenation.

# Poison

In *Fasting and Eating for Health*, Joel Fuhrman, M.D., notes, p. 10: *"The fast does not merely detoxify; it also breaks down superfluous tissue—fat, abnormal cells, athermanous plaque, and tumors, and releases diseased tissues and their cellular products into the circulation for elimination. Toxic or unwanted materials circulate in our bloodstream and lymphatic tissues, and are deposited in and released from our fat stores and other tissues. An important element of fasting detoxification is mobilizing the toxins from their storage areas. This process occurs best and most efficiently during total fasting."*

> *"...So a curse without a cause does not alight."*
> *(Proverbs 26:2)*

Our bodies contain many billions of tiny cells and each one must be fed. Cells must also eliminate waste products. Periodic fasting creates an alkaline environment, which allows our bodies to expel these waste products and toxins we now accumulate at unprecedented rates. A person can develop rashes, pimples, or even boils as these toxic substances are released through the skin. Also, the liver, which is the body's primary filter, gets a chance to rest and clean itself out. Rest is good. Leviticus 25:1-7 informs us that even the land must be rested, as the Hebrews didn't plant any crops on the land on every seventh year. Today the farmers have discarded this principle in favor of rotation, and poisons accumulate in the fields day after day, year after year, as they do in our bodies.

We constantly ingest artificial flavoring, food coloring, additives, pesticides, fungicides, herbicides, insecticides, rancid oils, medications and incalculable chemicals. Toxins also come from bacteria, mold, yeast, hazardous waste, heavy metals, smog, waste disposal, cars, planes, factories, and the list goes on. We're polluted daily by greedy food processors who sell us devitalized foods. We're poisoned by factories, cars and agribusiness. We accumulate toxins through water, food and through the air we breathe. There's no escape. Scientists have discovered poisons are carried by winds to and from the remotest places on the planet. In 1993 alone, more than 1,672,127,735 pounds of toxic chemicals were released into our air, according to the Environmental Protection Agency's Toxic Release Inventory of 1993, (www.epa.gov/triexplorer/chemical.htm.)

While walking down a city street, I noticed a man spraying chemicals designed to kill dandelion on a very tidy lawn. I find it very perplexing that we kill a seed bearing herb, whose roots and leaves are filled with beneficial vitamins and other properties while we poison the perimeter of our homes. We walk on these lawns, along with our children and pets, and the poisons are tracked into our homes, into our carpets, and eventually into us. Our cities have massive spray programs to kill mosquitoes and other bugs. We spray along roadways to kill weeds. Farmers spray plants. Pest control people spray in and around our homes. And we wonder why disease is on the rise.

If a person feels run down, tired, and unable to function with normal energy, they may simply be suffering from toxemia. There are so many mysterious illnesses these days. Many first manifest in one's weakest organs, thus the myriad of symptoms and confusing or non-existent medical diagnosis. At this early stage of contamination, the body's organs are barely able to expel and deal with these toxins. We may experience memory loss, depression, psychosis, anxiety, and many other forms of mental illness. Once the blood and organs become saturated and overwhelmed, toxins invade our cells and serious disease may follow like Parkinson's or cancer.

*"Autointoxication"* or toxic overload can be mental or spiritual. We're poisoned by movies, magazines, television, our own thoughts and other bad habits. I call it *the chemistry of sin.* Bad thoughts cause bad reactions. *"As a person thinks so they are." (Proverbs 23:7) (Paraphrased)*

Over many years toxins can accumulate in our bodies to hazardous levels. When stored on the cellular level they interfere with cell metabolism and regeneration. When toxins collect in cells, we age rapidly and the chance for disease increases. Our bodies have a limited capacity to handle poison. A normal adult can have from 5 to 10 pound of toxins locked in their tissues or organs. Healthy or not, we all have poisons in our bodies. A proper fast will remove them; otherwise a person may carry these poisons right into an early grave.

During a fast, we may or may not feel toxic release through various discomforts. It varies from person to person, depending on the health and strength of their constitution, the amount and types of toxins, where they're located, and where they travel. The following symptoms can be experienced: headaches, muscle aches, irregular heartbeat, dizziness, nausea, diarrhea, exhaustion, flu like symptoms, fever, cramps, hunger, bad breath, irregular menstruation, hot flashes, rash, eczema, skin odor and skin eruptions. This phenomenon or "symptomatic reversal of symptoms" is called a "healing crisis" and could last until the backlog of toxic material is reduced or eliminated. This healing process should be endured and viewed as beneficial. The alternative is using drugs that simply cover up the symptoms and pain while the inner deterioration continues.

There's a literal pharmacy within us. Fasting is a personal decision and the body will react with God-given, built-in inherent wisdom. The right attitude is important during a fast. A person should envision themselves healing, cleaning and becoming a better person. A person that envisions healing has a better chance to heal. Adequate rest is vital, for the body heals best during deep states of relaxation.

Dr. Deepak Chopra, author of *Perfect Health* says: *"When you fast, you rid yourself of ama (indigestible materials) which can*

*make your skin dull, your breath malodorous, and your joints achy.*
*You also rebalance your entire digestive system. It's like resetting*
*your thermostat."*

There are numerous other changes that occur during a fast.
During the first few days our pH balance becomes more alkaline
than acid, the stomach will shrink and the digestive tract is
cleansed. Initially, there'll be a protein loss of up to 75 grams a day,
compared to as little as 15-20 grams as the fast lengthens.
Germany's late Otto Buchinger, M.D., after supervising almost
90,000 juice-fasting "cures" eventually concluded in, *FASTING:*
*THE BUCHINGER METHOD*, page 22: *"The need for protein*
*diminishes during the fast, until in the second week, it has been*
*reduced from 100 grams to 15-20 grams a day, and this amount is,*
*in fact, quite sufficient while fasting."*

The diminished protein consumption is due to a slower
metabolism. As our bodies figure out they're not receiving food,
they automatically slow things down to conserve energy. (See
Chapter on Metabolism) As metabolism slows, the liver begins to
cleanse itself as the fast continues. Some people experience
frequent urination and bowel movements can vary or be nonexis-
tent. Concentration of toxins in the urine can be ten times more than
normal and the urine can be discolored.

# Warning

*"The simple believes every word, but the prudent man considers well his steps." Proverbs 14:15*

Common sense should always prevail. If symptoms become too severe during a fast, then caution should be taken. It's conceivable that someone releasing mercury or some other deadly toxin could be at risk. Generally speaking, most fasters will have no problem handling symptoms. But there'll be exceptions, and if a body contains too much poison, and the poison begins to flush into the system, there can be danger and the fast should be discontinued immediately.

Other symptoms that can arise during a fast include vertigo, cold extremities, feelings of sickness and depression, unstable sleep patterns, and some irritable memory and mental changes, such as forgetfulness and light-headedness. During a normal fast, enough liquid should be drunk, whether water or juice, to help dilute toxins as they make their way out of the body. Proper consultation and preparation is paramount for a serious fast, especially if a person is extremely toxic. (See Preparation and Detoxification Chapter)

Note: Before a person breaks a fast due to uncomfortable symptoms, they need know that such signs are natural and part of the healing process. There may be some discomfort, but this is normal in a healing crisis. Symptoms are a good sign that the fast is working. If the symptoms become overwhelming, a person should break the fast. At this point, the faster has already accomplished some good, though more poisons remain. They can assume a more gradual process of shorter fasts, and do a longer fast sometime in the future when their system is clearer. A person can also begin with short fasts and do them for a considerable length of time, in order to eliminate as much toxins as possible, then as the body clears, the fasts can be lengthened.

# Autolysis

*Dr. Otto Buchinger describes the entire process of fasting, as burning rubbish. He calls autolysis "refuse disposal".*

**A**utolysis, as it relates to fasting, is one of the <u>most</u> significant, compelling and encouraging scientific healing discoveries ever made! During a fast, the body in its instinctual wisdom begins to slowly burn all non-essential matter (impurities) in the body before it ever touches the vital muscles, organs and tissues. Autolysis is fire, an extension of body heat, normally 98.6 degrees. Since the body receives no food during a fast, the body will begin to search for nourishment and autolysis ensues, burning aged, morbid, damaged, or dead cells, fat, toxins, poisons, skin spots, calcium and mineral deposits in joints, superfluous fluids and mucous, reserve protein, undigested food, purines, metabolic wastes, abscesses, tumors, vitamins, free radicals, uric acid and all unhealthy and reserve tissue in the body. Are you excited yet? A human body is brilliantly designed to live on its own stored resources, as are other creatures such as bears and even insects. For example, a boa constrictor, weighing approximately 200 pounds, can survive on its own stored substance for up to a year between meals.

Fasting is like a refiner's furnace, burning impurities from our bodies. Autolysis, the fire in this furnace, finds and removes impurities first. When a silversmith desires to make a worthy vessel, they heat the silver over and over. During this process, the dross rises to the surface. The dross is then scooped off time and again, until the silver is pure and ready for fabrication. In our bodies the dross or impurities are expelled through the elimination organs.

Nobel Prize-winning biologist and surgeon Dr. Alexis Carrel, described in, *MAN, THE UNKNOWN*, the body's brilliant rejuvenate and regenerative capability, inherent in its own detoxification process during a fast: *"Privation of food at first brings a sensation of hunger, occasionally some nervous stimulation, but it also determines certain hidden phenomena which are more important. The sugar of the liver and the fat of the subcutaneous deposits are mobilized, and also the proteins of the muscles and the glands. . .in order to maintain blood, heart, and brain in a normal condition. Fasting purifies and profoundly modifies our tissues."*

We can also consider autolysis to be like a fever. When there's an impurity in the system, the body can naturally increase heat in order to burn away problem invaders. A fever is defense mechanism and can often the best thing that can happen. A fever is the detoxification process at work. A fever is forced, natural autolysis. Like the process employed by the silversmith who heats up the silver and scoops off impurities as they surface, so fasting is God's firepower, his refining furnace for our mind, bodies and souls.

*An unknown ancient physician said; "Give me the power to induce a fever and I will show you the way to cure all disease."* This statement may be bit exaggerated, but nonetheless intrinsically true. Similarly, fasting simply allows the body to use its own natural, internal heat to destroy problem invaders.

> *"What is to give light must endure burning."*
> *Viktor Frankl*

Other effects during a fast are a probable drop in blood pressure and heart rate and a certain loss in weight. Organs rest and the entire system is cleansed. As the body is relieved from its burden of normal functions like digestion and elimination, it'll clean, remove, sanitize, refurbish and renew its cells at a greater rate.

Cells are regenerated and renewed every year, as is every organ. If our bodies are renewed annually, then why do we continue to be in bad health? Why aren't we brand new every year? Why doesn't health return? The answer is simple. We overeat, maintain bad habits, and accumulate more toxins than the body can expel. Accumulation bogs down the entire system and we never feel better. Cells may be new, but they simply inherit the toxic overload or obese conditions and bad habits that were lodged in the old cells. And, science has yet to measure the subtle effects on our bodies from debilitating practices like pride, anger, unforgiveness, envy and hate.

When we eat more than the body can manage to deal with, we overload the digestive, assimilation and elimination systems. As with excess toxins, the body will store excess food in places most easily accessed. We all know where these places are, and we know the excess is called fat.

Statistics bear out the fact, that as we age, we become more susceptible to disease, the accumulation of toxins increases, metabolism slows and it becomes more difficult to lose weight. People that don't fast or never purify their bodies can eventually become overly toxic. Toxic saturation causes disease. How many of our elderly suffer needlessly with high blood pressure, diabetes, hypoglycemia, headaches, obesity and are on medications for the rest of their lives? What a way to live and we continue to buy the lies.

During a fast our elimination organs, the lungs, skin, kidneys, bowels, and our body's filter the liver, which stores much of the poison, remain active. Our entire system naturally and instinctively recognizes that it's fasting, and greatly increases the cleansing process. By removing toxins, we not only become healthier, but we remove blockages, allowing our energy to flow freer, and this includes increasing the heat of autolysis. Once our energy increases the cleansing and healing process also increases, and for once, we're on an upward spiral instead of the prevalent downward spirals we've all become accustomed to. Due to a more cleansed system, rested organs, additional energy and renewed vigor, our cells now rebuild at a faster rate. By fasting, our entire system can be transformed to its ultimate potential!

During a fast our resolve will be tested. Our determination, patience, stamina and focus may be challenged like never before. Fasting puts a person into the very trenches of life, on the front lines of battle on every level. When resolve is attacked, and when fasting is difficult, we need only remind ourselves of the myriad of benefits and of what's happening inside. We need to visualize, and to have faith in how we'll feel when we're purified and rejuvenated. *"For we walk by faith, not by sight." (2 Cor. 5:7)* We need to realize that minute-by-minute, toxins are being released. After the initial hunger pains diminish any hunger we may feel will subside, until the body eventually tells us the fast is really over.

# Water Fasting

Water is needed by every living thing, and second to air, it's our most important nutrient. Water comprises 65%-75% of an adult body, even 33% of bones. Water comprises up to 90% of a baby's body. It's a universal solvent which acts as a tiny magnet with a positive and negative charge. It's used continually by the body and needs to be replenished often. If we lost 20% of our body's water, we could die. Without water, we can't live for more than a few days.

In an average lifetime, a person drinks around 7,000 gallons, or 58,333 pounds of water. It's the major ingredient in foodstuffs and the common denominator of all liquids. It exists in every cell of the body and blood. It lubricates our joints and limbs, aids digestion and regulates temperature. It's essential for stimulation, circulation and elimination, and also helps in the absorption process. Every chemical process in the body happens in a water based solution.

Most health authorities agree that we should drink an average of ten 6 ounce glasses of water a day. During a fast it's important to drink a lot of water, no less than one large glass every half hour, to help flush out loosened impurities. Make sure the water is pure. Premium drinking water should contain no contaminants, no calories and nothing artificial. If we don't drink enough water, the organs of the body will begin to malfunction.

Historically, the only pollutants mankind had to worry about were organic organisms and debris like dirt, leaves and sand, but today we live in contact with over fifteen thousand chemicals that are on the market. Five hundred more are added yearly. Regardless of where we live, chemicals get into drinking water. No one on earth can determine the results of these chemicals in our bodies. And what happens when these chemicals inadvertently combine into untold harmful variations? Americans alone eat up to five pounds of chemicals in an average lifetime. The chemical industry produces 12 million tons of chlorine a year. Chlorine is foreign to our bodies, and used in a variety of products, in swimming pools and spas and in all city drinking water. Humans, fish, and wildlife are all affected.

We must become more aware of the quality of drinking water. Most of the toxins mankind releases eventually end up in our water. Undrinkable water has become epidemic. According to *Diet for a Poisoned Planet*, less than one percent of the earth's surface water is safe to drink in its present state. Public Health officials regularly find that 10%-40% of all private wells are contaminated with bacteria, agricultural chemicals and other pollutants. If you want to know what's in your water, you can have your tap or well water tested by private or public sources.

Municipal water is monitored for contaminants under the provisions of the *Safe Water Drinking Act*. They stay on the lookout for certain chemicals, but newly discovered and unrecognizable chemicals are now increasingly found in our water. When most water treatment plants were built they didn't have to deal with the myriad of new chemicals and combinations. The chlorine and aluminum our treatment plants use to purify the water stays in the water.

The urinary system controls, regulates and removes the water in our systems. During a fast, a person can bottle and examine their urine. The color, smell and inclusions will help indicate the condition of the body. During the fast water is ingested in a pure form and eliminated after it collects toxins and waste products released by the body. Urine can be stored in a clear jar. Poisons and other impurities within the urine will crystallize in a couple of days. The famous fasting proponent, Dr. Bragg, saved his urine everyday during a ten day fast and had it analyzed. He once found traces of the deadly poison DDT. How wonderful it would be to remove such a poison from the system.

Water fasting is the purest form of a fast, flushing toxins and poisons from the body rapidly and aggressively. When the body doesn't receive enough water, toxins tend to stagnate and settle in different areas, hindering all metabolic processes.

Water fasting gives the body no other option but to turn to its reserves for fuel. This could create a problem if we have spent years depositing counterfeit fuel. If we're very toxic and fasting for purely physical cleansing, we can ease into water fasting by drinking juice with shorter periods of water fasting. For example: 3 days on juice, 2 days on water, 5 days on juice, then 3 days on water.

Many influential people in history were humble. Moses was considered the most humble man on earth and also a great leader. The opposite of humility is pride, which is a weakness, a cover-up for spiritual famine within. Water fasting strips away cover-ups and shows us our deep need for humility. Fasting is an attitude of humility before God, a time to remember just how dependant we are on Him. We're fragile flesh and during water fasting we taste that frailness.

Water fasting totally contradicts the high-octane rush of the Western lifestyle. It's a period of brokenness, humility and profound inner reflection. Jesus fasted 40 days in the desert on water alone as he prepared for His confrontation with the world. Water fasting is a preparation to face worldly entrapments and evil forces with a brand new perspective. Everything is stripped to its bare essentials and things that really matter come to the forefront.

During such a fast it's important to use pure, uncontaminated water. Otherwise, we defeat a good part of our purpose. Bottled water is regulated by the FDA as a food. Emphasis is on sanitation and absence of bacteria at the bottling plant, using about the same guidelines as tap water. Often bottled water is labeled natural, which may mean it's not treated at all, just taken from a spring. You have to read the label.

Filtration removes sediment and particles from water and is the most basic treatment. Activated Carbon Treatment involves passing water through activated carbon, improving taste, color and purity.

Neither filtration nor the activated carbon system is very effective in removing minerals. Deionization is a process which uses ion exchange to produce very high quality water. Reverse Osmosis is the process where water is forced through a very thin membrane to remove dissolved minerals.

Distilled water is chemical and mineral free, consequently it's sometimes called dead or unstructured water. The body does need minerals, but they needn't come from water. There are plenty of good minerals in natural food. The perceived value of mineral water is misleading because the inorganic minerals are like huge boulders to the cellular membranes, often making them impossible to assimilate. Plants are able to break down the minerals from the soils, allowing them to be completely absorbed by the cells of the body.

A water distiller removes almost everything from water by boiling the water, collecting the steam, then condensing it. If done correctly, distilled water should be of the highest quality and it's the best for cleansing because of its inherent magnetic properties and ability to absorb and suspend large quantities of toxins and flushing them from the body. The best water is distilled, secondly, spring or filtered. If you want to buy processed bottled water which has most of the dissolved minerals removed, you should look for water that has been treated by Deionization, reverse osmosis or distillation, and then settle on the brand that tastes best. Water can pick up bacteria and the taste of the plastic container if it sits too long. Check shelf life.

It's not advisable to water fast under severe health conditions. But in the long run, God rules over all physical conditions. Hence, if you're called by God to water fast in spite of how foolish and irrational it may seem, obey God; just make sure it's Him.

Whether fasting or not, each person should drink sufficient water, at least the minimum daily average requirement of 6 to 8 glasses a day. Make sure the water is of high quality!

# Juice Fasting

W ater fasting proponents say, that in the strictest sense, juice fasting is no more than a liquid diet. Dr. Paavlo Airola and Dr. Buchinger, both juice fasting advocates and considered clinical experts on the subject, suggest that for healing, detoxification and rejuvenation, juice fasting is far superior to water fasting. They suggest that since *autolysis* also occurs during a juice fast, it should be considered a legitimate fast. They also emphasize that juice fasting has been clinically proven to promote and speed healing. They claim rejuvenation is sped up on the cellular level, because juice helps better eliminate dead and dying cells, along with other waste products. Scripture tells us that seed bearing herbs are given for our healing. Juice fasters may have inadvertently stumbled onto another divine precept.

Juices contain a high percentage of water, which is biologically active, in that it contains nutrients essential to our health, such as enzymes, vitamins, minerals and trace elements that actually aid the body in its curative process, as well as help eliminate and neutralize toxins. Different vegetables, fruits, and broth have assorted minerals and vitamins, which in turn have various results on different organs. Generally, fruit contains the most water, vegetables slightly less. Carrots for example contain up to 88% water.

During a fast, we normally absorb up to 90% of these nutrients. Juices are assimilated directly into our systems without stimulating and activating the entire digestive process. Due to the fact that organs and bodily processes rest during a fast, juices are assimilated and utilized by the body with little or no digestive energy. Experts claim that the utilization of nutrients is more complete, since there's little other activity or interference from food.

Dr. Ragnar Berg, one of the most respected biochemical and nutritional authorities says: *"During fasting the body burns up and excretes huge amount of accumulated wastes. We can help this cleansing process by drinking alkaline juices instead of water while fasting. I have supervised many fasts and made extensive tests of fasting patients and I am convinced that drinking alkaline forming fruit and vegetable juices, instead of water during fasting will increase the healing effect of fasting. Elimination or uric acid and other inorganic acids will be accelerated. And, sugars in juice will strengthen the heart. Juice fasting is, therefore, the best form of fasting."*

Juice fasting is easier than water fasting, in that there is some nutrition. Dick Gregory made headlines when he ran fifteen miles on the 100th day of a juice fast.

### Common Juices Ideal for a Fast

| | | | |
|---|---|---|---|
| Carrot | Apple | Beet | Celery |
| Cucumber | Tomato | Alfalfa | Vegetable Broth |
| Garlic | Spinach | Lemon | Papaya |
| Cabbage | Asparagus | Pineapple | Orange |
| Pear | Grape | Grapefruit | Cinnamon tea |
| Ginger Tea | Chamomile | Wheat Grass | Peppermint |
| Spearmint | Wheatgrass | Watermelon | Green Pepper |
| Cherry | Cranberry | Pear | Prune |
| Aloe Vera | Parsley | Garlic | Lettuce |
| Nectarines | Lime | Berries | |

To make fresh, organic juice, fruits or vegetables should be cleaned and juiced. Find a juicer with a strong motor, one that's easily cleaned, easy to use and reasonably priced. Excellent brands are Champion, Phoenix, Acme 6001 and Omega. Juices should be drunk as soon as possible. In their freshest state they contain optimum vitality. Stored juice should be kept cold.

Herbs can be added to juice for various effects. (See Chapter on Herbs) Essential minerals such as magnesium, zinc, calcium, sulfur, iodine, potassium, silicon, iron, and trace elements like kelp, nettles, horsetail, Irish moss, yellow dock and watercress are positive additions to juice.

There's an ongoing controversy on the differences between water and juice fasting, but I believe fasting will be beneficial either way. When herbal healing enters the picture through juice fasting, there's ample credibility, since we find that herbs are recommended for healing in cultures around the world. No matter which fast you are led to do, or which fast you're more comfortable with, the idea here is to fast and realize the profound benefits.

Freshly-squeezed and extracted fruit and vegetable juices, broth and herbal teas supply vitamins, minerals, live enzymes and other organically-complex nutrients that promote healing during the fast. By providing much of the body's daily caloric needs with the easily-absorbed juices, the release of toxins from the fat cells is much more gradual and gentle. Juices will also supply the 400 calories or so that's your minimal fuel requirement. What's more, fresh juices have a cleansing effect of their own, and if they're taken immediately after being made, they're energizing and exhilarating.

Juice is a living fuel that takes no digestive energies from the body, allowing the body's major focus to be on healing and rejuvenation. Juice is low enough in calories to still force the body to cannibalize on its filthy waste. During juice fasting, there may still be periods of toxic crisis, but once you learn not to fear them, they can bring an exciting anticipation that your body is going through a deep cleansing. Signs of premature aging, loss of interest in sex and a bulging waistline, all obvious signs of insufficiently functioning endocrine or sex glands and diminished sex-hormone production are usually reversed during juice-fasting.

The best juices are fresh lemon (unless kidneys are overly polluted), cabbage, beet, carrot, celery, grape, apple, wheat grass, barely grass and green drinks made from leafy vegetables. These are excellent detoxifiers. Raw cabbage juice is known to help heal ulcers, cancer and colon problems. However, it must be fresh, not stored, as it loses vitamin content if stored for too long. An excellent therapeutic blend is the juice from three carrots, two stalks of celery, one turnip, two beets, a half head of cabbage, a quarter bunch of parsley and a clove of garlic.

Chlorophyll products are excellent because they oxygenate the blood, build hemoglobin similar to iron, and increase healing and detoxification. Barley Green juice is an excellent source of enzymes and is high in chlorophyll. Wheat grass is less convenient and less tolerable in flavor, but an excellent source of chlorophyll and trace minerals.

Pure vegetable broth, with no seasonings is also good for fasting. To prepare, gently boil veggies, including garlic, for 30 minutes. Strain the broth through a cloth and drink two to three times a day. Watermelon fasts in season, or fresh carrot or grape juice also make fine fasting juices. If you must eat something (not recommended) have a slice of watermelon (in season). Always eat watermelon alone. Organic grapes or fresh apple sauce made with the skins on and processed in a blender are satisfying and won't significantly disrupt your fast.

# The Grape Fast

There's a sanitarium in Yalta, Russia specializing exclusively in grape fasts. Patients begin by eating one pound of fresh grapes and work up to ten pounds per day. Besides detoxifying the body and curing intestinal ailments, grapes greatly enhance metabolism and strengthen the heart muscle. There have been a number of patients that have credited the grape fast with curing terminal cancer. Anyone suffering from cancer should obtain a book entitled *The Grape Cure* by Johanna Brandt. *The Grape Cure* is founded on personal experience and though it advocates prevention, Johanna cured herself of terminal, inoperable cancer. To those so afflicted, the grape fast may present a final hope.

*Before starting on the grape diet, it's absolutely essential to remove any and all prejudice from our minds and hearts. Start with a clean sheet, then the only thing you will have to eradicate is the obstruction in your physical body. (Johanna Brandt, Pretoria, S.A. Chapter 1 - The Fourth of July, 1927)*

The history and tradition found in the simple grape is long and diverse. There are between 40 and 50 different varieties of grapes which come in a multiple of greens, whites, reds and purples. In earliest history, grapes were considered the food of gods. They were found in Egyptian tombs and ancient writings are filled with stories about the joys and sorrows resulting from its fermented juices. Grape production and wine-making are steeped in tradition and secrecy. Grapes fill the mouth with an explosion of delicious flavors. They are an excellent source of potassium which encourage an alkaline blood balance and also stimulate the kidneys and regulate the heart beat. The restorative power of grapes is phenomenal, from cleansing the liver to removing uric acid from the body.

Grapes are the most overly-sprayed fruit, therefore if you're not sure they're organic, wash thoroughly. Always look for a faint powdery appearance, indicating blooming. A grape bunch should have a few grapes either falling off or mushy. The stems should not be shriveled, but green-looking. Grapes keep for a week in the refrigerator. Raisins are also a wonderful, healthy substitute for candy and a good source of iron.

In France, many people go on an annual grape-fast during harvest time. Studies have shown a lower incidence of cancer in the areas of France where this grape-fast occurs regularly. Grapes with seeds are recommended for this fast. Grapes also make excellent juice, although they make the juicer sound like a miniature machine gun. Don't worry, the juicer won't be damaged. Make sure you swirl the juice in your mouth before swallowing. If you drink too quickly, there'll not be enough saliva for proper digestion, which may cause stomach cramps. (This is good advice for all juice fasting) If you find grape juice too sweet, add some lemon juice. It can also be mixed half and half with water if the juice is too strong.

The proanthocyanidins and gallicesters, which are found only in grape seed extract, enhance the power of vitamins C and E, strengthen capillaries, enhance circulation, improve eyesight, restore skin elasticity and softness, and block blood platelet and LDL oxidation. At the turn of the century, Johanna Brandt wrote that *"Grapes seem to ferret out the most deep-seated cause of trouble and drive it from the system."* This is an excellent book and I highly recommend it if you are suffering from cancer or any other disease, or if you simply would like to learn more about the marvels of the grape fast.

# Things to Do During a Fast

*"Finally brethren, whatever things are true, whatever things are noble, whatever things are just, whatever things are pure, whatever things are lovely, whatever things are of good report, if there be any virtue, and if there is anything praiseworthy, meditate on these things. The things which you learned and received and heard and saw in me, these do, and the God of peace will be with you." (Philippians 4:8-9)*

For the most part, I personally maintain a normal schedule during a fast. Not everyone will be able to do this, and depending on the type of fast attempted, a person may need to find a quiet natural place to heal or commune with God.

*"...for the world is mine and all its fullness."*
*(Psalm 50:12)*

There are many positive things we can do to enhance our fasting experience. It's a perfect time to read. Prayer and fasting are a most effective combination during a fast. Music can be relaxing and soothing. Mild sun bathing is an invigorating tonic, charging us with beneficial energies. Our bodies are like human solar panels, as the millions of tiny nerve endings collect vitamin D from the sun. A moderate amount of sunshine provides energy, relaxation and has been proven to enhance the overall effectiveness of our senses. We obtain sunshine indirectly when we eat, as sun develops chlorophyll (the blood in plants and herbs), which is like liquid sunshine. Sunshine should be taken in moderation and increased only as the body develops darker pigment. Folk wisdom in India maintains that the morning sun gives energy, while the afternoon sun drains energy.

*"Plan your work, and then work your plan."*
*J. Lazur*

Showers are great during a fast and can be alternated between hot and cold to stimulate circulation. A warm bath helps calm emotions and soothes nerves. If you can access a natural hot springs, it's a treat. There are approximately 2 million sweat glands in the skin, and even without heavy perspiration, we lose between 1/2 to 2 1/2 pints of water daily. If we combined these sweat glands they would create a tube about twelve inches in diameter. During a whirlpool, steam or sauna, the body can drain up to ten times this amount. Remember to drink lots of water.

An abdominal massage can be beneficial during a fast. During a massage, oil can be rubbed into the skin to soften it and to help healing. Before a massage, bathing and vigorously brushing the skin using a dry vegetable, natural bristle brush helps stimulate and clean skin.

A person can continue working, as long as the work is not overly strenuous. Good rest is indispensable, and so is exercise. Exercise and fasting go together. If we don't use our muscles, they'll atrophy, or in other words, shrink and weaken. Mild exercise is usually recommended, like swimming, biking, gymnastics, and dancing, deep breathing exercises and especially walking. My favorite exercises are walking and swimming, as both are smooth, relaxing and exhilarating. These exercises are great for the lungs, skin tone, circulatory system and heart. Fasting is simple, and there's no need to complicate or overdo matters. Overly strenuous exercise is discouraged. The body should not be overly stressed as fasting is a healing and resting time. Common sense should prevail.

# Metabolism

*"A strong body makes a strong mind."*
*Thomas Jefferson*

The digestive process kicks in when one begins to chew. Food mixes with saliva and begins to break down. Soon after food is swallowed, it's deposited in the stomach where contractions mix it with gastric juices, acids called pepsin, rennin and proteinase. After mixing, food makes its way to the small intestine, where it again mixes with bile from the liver, natural bacteria and intestinal juices. After it is mixed, food is absorbed through the intestinal walls where it's picked up by the blood vessels, and transported and assimilated into various parts of the body. The remains are processed by the liver and moved to the large intestine (colon), where they're compacted into solid waste to be eliminated through the rectum.

Metabolism, which varies according to genetics, fitness, activities, age and climate, is the rate with which we process and regulate bodily functions. Metabolism is bodily balance and delicate chemistry. When a person is unhealthy, metabolism is sluggish. Lack of proper nourishment will slow metabolism and harm the entire system. A healthy person has a balanced metabolism that takes from the blood what it needs to feed or repair cells.

The body needs high quality natural food to function at its

optimum and to properly regulate metabolism. When we subject our bodies to an excess of hard to digest food like meats, eggs and other heavy foods, we clog the system, and eventually it bogs down. Intoxication, toxins, junk food and malnutrition all alter chemistry. When our metabolic effectiveness is slowed we become prone to disease. When we fast, the body changes its metabolic speed. While we're eating, the body always eliminates and purifies, but during a fast the body no longer has to deal with incoming nutrients or outgoing waste, so it focuses all its energies on sanitizing.

In order to survive during the fast, the body begins to consume itself. Initially the body consumes only unwanted debris. As we've learned, this process is called autolysis. If we fast too long, the body would eventually begin to eat its cells, muscles, and other vital organs, and we'd starve. During starvation, metabolism comes to a virtual standstill. Pulse, temperature and blood pressure drop. As these functions become weak, the body turns cold. Starvation causes one to lose their sex drive, skin to dry, hair to fall out and eyes to bulge. A starving person usually dies when they lose approximately one third to one half of their body weight. We see the terrible effects of starvation in different parts of our planet. It's a travesty that people in our day and age starve with the overabundance of food available in some countries. When the metabolism of large groups of people comes to a halt for lack of food, we call it a famine.

Fasting and starvation are entirely different. The body intuitively recognizes and adjusts naturally to a fast. When the body figures out its not receiving food, organs slow to conserve energy, protein consumption automatically slows and our metabolism changes gears. The body knows exactly what to do, when to do it and how to do it. As the metabolism slows for the period of the fast, the body also lets a person know when the fast is over. When the person begins to eat, the metabolism will return to its previous level.

There are many examples of people that have starved themselves to death as a form of political protest. In Ireland during the early 1900's, to protest British rule, Thomas Ashe fasted till death. Terrance MacSwiney fasted for 69 days then purposely died to accentuate his cause. Cesar Chavez advocated fasting in the

Spanish labor disputes. Many others stopped eating during these protests and eventually died.

As the metabolism slows during a fast, the liver automatically begins to cleanse itself. To keep the metabolism in peak form, the liver, gallbladder, and kidneys need to be stimulated and healthy. Exercise helps to maintain proper metabolism. Herbs can also stimulate the metabolism, such as cayenne, ginger, garlic, cloves, black pepper, as can the minerals manganese, iodine and amino acids. Herbal stimulants can restore or induce enough vitality to kick-start an ailing organ, aid digestion, or generally perk up a sluggish system. Stimulating herbs also break down blockages in the system as well as heat the body. Heating the body increases the intensity of autolysis. Herbs with heat inducing properties raise metabolism, while cooling herbs lower it.

There are several metabolic alterations as the body downshifts during a fast. If we only lived off stored protein, we would not live long, perhaps a week. After three to five days into a fast, our metabolism changes. The liver begins to convert fat to water-soluble molecules called ketones, which help keep the brain functioning. This phenomenon seems to coincide with the alleviation of hunger during a fast. Experts believe ketones may be responsible for the physical phenomenon of fasting. Ketones are found to be at maximum efficiency near the two-week mark of a fast. The body also reduces secretions and most people need less sleep.

An obese person can fast a long time as the body cannibalizes fat deposits. At the same time, muscles, organs and vital tissues are protected. With the change of metabolism, the body also protects protein in vital organs like the heart, kidneys, and brain. After about three weeks the body needs 20% less calories than it does when a person eats.

# Herbs

*"The Lord hath created medicines out of the earth;
and he that is wise will not abhor them."*
*(Ecclesiasticum 34:4)*

Every religion, as well as science, agrees we should apply the principal of fasting to our lives. We've learned that fasting helps us access deeper levels of health, but we needn't stop there. We can apply other principles and be even more effective. With proper knowledge we can obtain all the bounty and blessing available to us. When concerned with overall well-being, we'd be missing out if we didn't consider the benefits of herbs.

*"He (God) causes the grass to grow for the cattle
and herbs for the service of humanity." (Psalms
104:14) (Parenthesis added)*

Nature can be appreciated for its beauty, its glorious plant life, vibrant colors, aromas and sheer variety. How bland and different our lives would be without flowers and how tasteless our meals would be without spices. Herbs and spices enhance the flavor of our food, as well as being highly nutritious. They protect our gardens, sweeten our air, beautify our environment, stimulate our senses and refresh our souls. But the plants about us are more than beauty and more than food. They're God's pharmacy. If we search history, we learn every culture and generation has benefited from plants. Herbs are medicine for our diseases.

> *"Excellent herbs had our fathers of old, excellent*
> *Herbs to ease their pain, alexanders and marigold,*
> *eyebright, orris, and elecampane." Rudyard Kipling*

There are valuable resources in plant life. Herbs help cleanse, normalize, feed, energize and stimulate the bodily system. Herbs have a curative history of encouraging, purifying, and supporting blood, tissues, organs, cells and cleaning bowels. The essence of herbal therapy, like fasting, is to activate the body's own miraculous self-healing powers. Herbs do not heal. Herbs assist the healing process.

Herb, from the Latin word for grass, is any useful plant used for medicine. Outside the Western world's profit centered environment, much of the earth's population still utilizes herbal medicine. Every culture uses herbs and puts them into food or drink for culinary purposes, flavoring, and health reasons.

Natural healing properties in herbs are the same today as they were in ancient times. Throughout history, herbal remedies were selected from tradition, observation, and experience and handed down by word of mouth as well as in written works. Those skilled in their use became valued members of society. Like never before, our vast communication abilities have provided us with the select advantage of being able to access global information almost immediately. Though more could be done, herbal knowledge, once held as secret or obscured in primitive societies, is now subject to scientific study as well as increased clinical data and experience.

When sick or out of balance, the whole body is not affected, but the crisis is most often localized, such as a headache, sore throat, or maybe our joints ache. The body has buffer zones that keep infection or sickness from spreading. Only glands or a particular organ may be affected. We can find the specific herb or combination of herbs to help heal or balance the particular area in need. Specific areas will react to specific herbs.

*"Every plant that My Father has not planted will be uprooted." (Matthew 15:13)*

If we analyze medicinal herbs, we'll find only small amounts of nutrients. The active ingredients are alkaloids or organic compounds that can alter the metabolism of the body. Medical research continues to update their evaluations. More needs to be done, and plants need to be protected from extinction. There may be an herb somewhere to help with every disease. Herbs are allies, our helpers. Herbs feed and regulate organs, bolster the immune system, reduce cholesterol, provide minerals, enzymes, oils, resins, mucilage and target specific glands. Herbs act on and protect the blood, improve circulation, regulate metabolism and other life's processes, including the nervous system. Herbs can help prevent disease.

*"An ounce of prevention is worth a pound of cure."*
*Author unknown*

*"And the fruit thereof shall be meat, and the leaf thereof for medicine." (Ezekiel 47:12)*

Nearly half of our present-day medications are synthetic reproductions of natural plants. For example, Aspirin was synthesized from a natural pain-relieving compound found in White Willow bark. Herbs have a therapeutic effect because they either adjust the body's healing mechanism or stimulate a cleansing reaction. Herbs often have a specific effect that can benefit various organs. Herbs work in alignment with the body, rarely causing side effects. Conversely, chemicals and synthetic medications ignore the body's natural balance, and often cause side effects and deposit chemicals that can stay lodged in our tissues for years. Chemical medicines are notorious for their side effects, stimulating healing in one area of the body while having a negative effect on the whole system.

All through ancient times, we find people that chewed and brewed plants around them, and through trial and error, learned their specific benefits and uses. They used seeds, flowers, leaves, stems, fruits, roots, bark, wood, resin, gum, latex extraction, essential oils and nuts of plants. And this wasn't just one race of people in one particular place, or in one era, but in almost every culture throughout history. Such accumulated knowledge becomes even more remarkable when we understand that cultures removed from one another by oceans and by vast time spans often arrived at some of the same conclusions involving the same type of herbs.

Today, herbs are more revered and highly regarded in some parts of the world than others. Chinese are expert in the use of herbs and have recorded their uses for some 3600 years. Legend has it that an ancient Chinese emperor began to catalog herbs thousands of years ago. He experimented with them and recorded their effects. The emperor eventually died when he ingested a poisonous plant, but he's still credited with compiling the first herb book.

When the Europeans settlers came to the North American shores, they were confronted with many hardships, harsh winters and sickness. Native Americans introduced them to healing herbs that are household names today, such as chamomile, slippery elm bark, lobelia, sarsaparilla, golden seal, cascara sagrada, and wild cherry, among others. The white men marveled at the Indian's effectiveness in dealing with wounds. Out of necessity they learned the art of herbal medicine.

Like fasting, herbal use isn't some magical potion or quick fix that'll immediately change our chemistry or remove pain. Their purpose is to aid healing, and to help bring the natural God-given chemistry into balance and optimum working order. The use of herbs must be applied with accurate and consistent knowledge, matching herbal properties with symptoms and combined with good habits and a sensible diet. A rule of thumb is to extend treatment one month for every year a disease has been developing. With proper application specific herbs will have their desired effect.

An herbal program undertaken before a fast can help detoxify the body and help set up the renewal experience. Herbs taken after fasting will be potent and accelerated, as the body has been cleaned, rejuvenated and eagerly awaiting nutrients.

Herbs can be gathered, cultivated, or purchased. Though herbal traditions vary somewhat, it's not too difficult to find uniformity and someone with proper herbal knowledge. As we've noted, with growing Internet communication capabilities we can access world-wide information quickly. There's also fairly consistent and adequate information available from one herb book to another.

Herbs are curative, aromatic, antibiotic, preventative and preservative. For certain, specific ailments, I recommend in-depth study and consultation before embarking on serious use. There's a myriad of plants available with healing properties, but sadly, mankind is destroying them quickly. In the Amazon Rain Forest, which is the very lungs of our planet, greed is rampant, and plant species are disappearing at an alarming and unprecedented rate.

For the most part, the Federal Drug Administration and the American Medical Association ignore herbs and herbology in favor of pharmaceuticals and synthesized vitamins. There has been an ongoing conspiracy and lobby to keep drug profits flowing. Most holistic doctors will tell you that the synthetic drugs prescribed for the most part only cover symptoms and often cause more problems than they solve. Our bodies don't need and don't know how to process synthetic ingredients, as the body has its own facility to make vitamins from the food and herbs we eat. If a person lacks essential vitamins they need to reevaluate their diet and add the proper herbs to wholesome foodstuff. Eat right, take the right herbs, and the body will take care of all its vitamins, minerals, and enzymes.

There's little or no benefit in taking synthetic vitamins being dispensed by the billions. They're virtually useless and can even be harmful. Though their producers often claim these pills to be natural, this claim is often misleading. So-called vitamins may contain natural ingredients, but they're merely extractions from the plant that are broken down, heated, and mixed with other ingredients. The heat and manufacturing process destroys most nutrients, and when the plant is broken down, its initial function is partially or completely destroyed. Most of the vitamins commonly found on the market should be avoided. They will only provide a person with subtle side effects and expensive urine. The properties of vitamins and minerals that the body needs are found in plants in their proper dosage and in their proper combinations. The following herbs and oils are a just few examples of plants that can be added to the diet if a person needs to achieve vitamin supplementation. Extensive lists can be found in many reputable herb books.

- <u>Vitamin A</u>: Cayenne, Red Clover, Yarrow, Yellow Dock, Alfalfa, Cohosh, Eyebright, Dandelion leaves, Stinging Nettles, Parsley, Savoy Cabbage, Carrots
- <u>Vitamin B</u>: Licorice, Cascara Sagrada, Fenugreek, Hawthorne, Papaya, Blue Cohosh, Cress, and Parsley
- <u>Vitamin C</u>: Rose Hips, Peppermint, Golden Seal, Juniper Berries, Chickweed, Comfrey, Echinacea, Garlic, Bee Pollen, Engadine berries,
- <u>Vitamin D</u>: Alfalfa, Sarsaparilla, Rose Hips, Red Raspberry, Dandelion, Cod liver oil, Carrot Juice
- <u>Vitamin E</u>: Burdock, Yarrow, Kelp, Ding Quai, Slippery Elm, Skullcap, and Wheat Germ Oil
- <u>Vitamin F</u>: Slippery Elm, Red Raspberry
- <u>Vitamin K</u>: Gota Kula, Yarrow, and Alfalfa
- <u>Calcium</u>: Carrots, White Oak Bark, Sage, Chamomile, Cayenne, Aloe, Fennel, Marshmallow, Kohlrabi, Celery leaves, White turnips, Swedes, Parsnips
- <u>Iodine</u>: Kelp, Bladderwrack
- <u>Magnesium</u>: Wood Betony, Alfalfa, Valerian, Rosemary, Red Clover, Gota Kola, Ginger, Catnip
- <u>Potassium</u>: Cascara Sagrada, Cayenne, Blue Cohosh, Aloe, Chaparral, Golden Seal, Fennel, Parsley, Slippery Elm, Yarrow, Rose Hips, Carrots
- <u>Zinc</u>: Hawthorne, Marshmallow, Sarsaparilla, Licorice, Chamomile, Burdock, Dandelion, and Eyebright
- <u>Trace Minerals</u>: (Found in all herbs) Rose Hips, Alfalfa, Burdock, Dandelion, Chaparral, Cascara Sagrada, Black Cohosh, Yellow Tail, Valerian Sage, Sarsaparilla, Lobelia, Parsley, Red Clover, Horsetail, Kelp

Herbs don't suppress or cover up the effects of illness, as is the case with many pharmaceuticals, but work to balance, clean, and activate our systems. Pharmaceuticals can actually interfere with the healing processes, and can cause serious harm. And why are these pills being sold to us?

> *"For the love of money is the root of all kinds of
> evil..." (I Timothy 6:10)*

Drug companies don't want to invest millions in herbal research, since anyone can grow them in their gardens or simply pick them, and of course, they have their present drug profit center in high gear. They spend mega dollars on advertising and a fraction of that amount on research. Pharmaceuticals are poisoning people and wreaking havoc. A recent report by the Health and Human Services Division estimates that 243,000 elderly are admitted to the hospital every year for adverse reactions to pharmaceuticals. Another 163,000 are estimated to develop mental disorders from these same so-called safe drugs whose side effects have run the gamut from unpleasant to lethal.

Tradition and experience tell us which herbs can be used safely for which benefit. Though herbs are perfectly safe, indiscriminate use isn't recommended. There are also poisonous plants and herbs that can and must be used in moderation. Most of us have read the story of Socrates and how he drank his infamous hemlock drink and died. Not only is it important to take the correct herb, but the correct amount, and for a reasonable period of time to insure proper healing and safety. Lack of commitment, knowledge and consistency are other major problems with herbal therapy. The fact that the drug companies control the marketplace and that their products are given safe status brings to light another problem we need to be aware of. There are those self-styled profit motivated people in the herbal industry as well, so be careful and use wisdom.

Insufficient or extreme dosage or a wrong diet can nullify herbal treatment. If a person is unsure and unfamiliar with herbs, it's wise to consult a reputable herb book or herbal specialist before undertaking such therapy.

Herbal formulas can be effective and have both primary and secondary effects. Herbs can detoxify, tone, stimulate, soothe, balance, calm, warm, cool, heal, dry, enhance virility, aid digestion, relieve stress, purge, pacify, or be added to the diet for prevention purposes. A mixture of herbs may be necessary as different organs may be affected by disease.

In developing herbal formulas, we classify herbs to help indicate their energetically dynamic properties, and how to best balance their combined use. Salty tasting herbs influence water balance, sweet herbs provide nutrition, pungent herbs disperse, sour herbs aid digestion and cooling, and bitter herbs cool and detoxify. Use of one herb for one effect is called a "Simple", but there are many blends and formulas for different results. Herbalists have long known and used combinations of herbs to aid healing and in rejuvenating techniques. To help give us an understanding of what an herbal formula is and how it works, we'll borrow from Chinese herbal tradition. We'll classify the herbs into four combinations that express primary and secondary functions:

1. Emperors: Emperors are powerful herbs that energize and stimulate the body and are the main ingredient in the formula.
2. Ministers: These are similar to the emperors, complimenting them, while they also tone and help herbal effects last longer.
3. Assistants: These herbs give balance to the formula and also give nourishment and a steadying effect. They also soothe the effects of stronger herbs.
4. Servants: These herbs combine with the other herbs to maximize their collective effectiveness. They act as a catalyst and help the body assimilate other herbs. Servants can also help reduce irritation.

Buy herbs from reputable sources. Make sure herbs are identified properly and never eat a strange herb. Use only recommended amounts and only for the time recommended. Common sense should prevail and a person should pay particular attention to severe symptoms if any occur. While using herbs for healing, it may be necessary to take large doses over a long period. A person should be careful when taking herbal oils, as they're concentrated and more powerful, but essential oils are the best form of herb, because when kept fresh, they have maximum potency. Dried herbs or herbal tablets dry out and lose potency, so it may be necessary to take higher dosages. All in all, herbs can usually be taken with no repercussions and no side effects.

I found it particularly interesting when I viewed detailed photos of the cross-section of the human cerebellum, the small part of the brain. It matched the pattern of a leaf. Curiously, the leaf is the most frequently used part of the herb, and its primary activity, photosynthesis, is fundamental to human existence. Photosynthesis actually forms the basis for our food chain. The chlorophyll found in leaves is antiseptic, clears toxins and is a basis for herbal healing.

# Fasting and Blood

*"For the life of the flesh is in the blood..."*
*(Leviticus 17:11)*

There are 100,000 miles of tubing throughout our bodies called veins. Connected, this transportation system would extend over two and one half times around the earth! In 1618 a scientist named Dr. Harvey discovered that blood flows. This was an extremely unpopular notion in his day and he was ridiculed and ostracized from the medical profession. Blood flows through this elaborate tubular system to protect us, to feed cells and to carry nutritious and healing energies so we may live.

*"A merry heart does good, like medicine."*
*(Proverbs 17:22)*

The heart, weighing approximately 11 ounces, pumps blood through this system at 2000 gallons a day! It increases blood flow to areas where healing occurs. Having a healthy circulation system is one of the most effective ways to promote healing. Everything we need, all necessary vitamins, minerals, amino acids, sugars, fats and oxygen are sent uninterruptedly through this network to each and every one of our billions of cells. One blood cell can make 3000 round trips around the body daily! If the blood becomes polluted, thoroughfares blocked, or flow reduced, we have a problem.

Toxins also flow through our bloodstream and end up in cells. They must be eliminated if the body is to function optimally. The blood stream is the basis of our purification system. Spiritually speaking, it's no coincidence that the pure blood of Jesus is the ingredient that cleanses sin. When blood is polluted and overburdened, we poison our cells and that eventually leads to disease. Blood tests are very effective in determining health. Scientist claim, that very soon everything about the body will be determined in analyzing one single drop of blood.

The best blood purifier we have at our disposal is fasting. Fasting cleans, purifies and recharges the five quarts of blood that's constantly moving in our veins. It was noted during the famous Swedish ten-day fast marches, that protein levels in the blood remained constant even though no nourishment was taken.

> *"But you shall not eat flesh with its life, that is, its blood." (Genesis 9:4) "...You shall not eat the blood of any flesh, for the life of all flesh is blood. Whoever eats it shall be cut off." (Leviticus 17:14)*

Also, taking another person's blood can be dangerous. There are at least 20,000 deaths a year in the US due to blood transfusions. Though transfusions seem to be necessary at times to save one's life, scientist still don't know the full implications of taking another's blood.

Hardening and narrowing of our arteries, no wider than a straw to begin with, have serious and often fatal consequences. If blood flow to the brain stops for even a minute or two, we can suffer a stroke or even die. Blockage happens slowly and silently. When blood flow is restricted to a certain degree, a person will quickly degenerate both physically and mentally. As the arteries constrict, the heart will not only work harder, but suffer from lack of nourishment. Sores develop and deposits build up, arteries lose elasticity, and they become brittle and blood pressure rises. This in turn puts pressure on the circulatory and immune system. There are natural ways to keep blood pressure down; and a fasting program is one of the best.

A natural diet is absolutely necessary for healthy arteries and to avoid heart attacks. A person can start by increasing grains, fibers, reduce fat intake and cut down on animal protein consumption. Cigarettes, coffee, alcohol and other heavy stimulants should be eliminated, as they also help narrow blood veins. Weight should be normalized.

Thin blood is safe blood. A sufficient supply of blood, along with thin blood, helps the entire circulatory system and is a key to health. Keeping blood thin minimizes the risk of heart attack, as the heart will not work as hard to pump thin blood, and the there's less likelihood of clots. Garlic, onion and vitamin E are excellent blood thinners. Though aspirin is said to thin blood, its use should be minimized or alleviated altogether, because it's an irritant. The heart is the hardest working organ in the body and needs to be cared for.

Bad habits that stress our blood and heart can be overcome by a fasting program. Herbs that help normalize blood pressure are capsicum, golden seal root, parsley, hawthorn, ginger, garlic, flaxseed oil, calcium and magnesium. To stimulate circulation one can use cayenne, juniper, peppermint, ginger, and angelica.

Toxins absorb into the bloodstream by way of the gastronomic tract entering through capillaries lining the colon wall. Once in the blood, the toxins can circulate throughout the body and may be absorbed into cells and skin, lowering our overall function and eventually setting the stage for disease. Toxins will accumulate in weaker areas of the body, where these impurities can then stagnate, clog the system and weaken the immune system. Blood must be purified. When toxic levels reach critical mass, some natural healers even recommend a small amount of blood letting to relieve pressure.

It's essential that blood get enough oxygen. Oxygen is the life of the blood, and if we don't get enough, toxins will accumulate faster. Exercise is the easiest and most natural way to oxygenate blood. Every heartbeat moves 2 1/2 ounces of blood with life-giving properties to our cells. Iron is the mineral to which oxygen attaches itself, so adequate iron is most essential. Nearly every food we eat contains iron and oxygen. Yellow Dock contains 40% iron and is an excellent herb and dietary supplement for the blood.

*"Every tissue in the body is fed by the blood, which is 90% water, and supplied by the intestines. When the intestines are dirty the blood is dirty and so are the organs and tissues. It is the intestinal system that must be cared for first before any effective healing can take place." Dr. Bernard Jensen*

Blood purification is the front line of health, and the immune system is the front guard in the war against disease. The immune system is comprised of over a trillion white blood cells designed to seek out and destroy invading microorganisms like bacteria, fungi, protozoa, viruses and other foreign substances. The white blood cells will mount an attack on anything that doesn't belong in the blood. White blood cells patrol the bloodstream, congregate around the enemy, neutralize it and destroy infected cells. These fighting white blood cells actually eat bacteria and kill impure material in an on-going inner battle for health. When a person fasts, they help eliminate these poisons, thereby giving these front line soldiers much needed rest. Take care of your precious army. During an elongated fast these warriors in our blood streams can be more effective and thoroughly destroy unwanted material in our blood!

Echinacea angustifolia is one of the strongest herbal blood purifiers. Additional blood purifying herbs are: burdock root, dandelion root, red clover, myrrh gum, golden seal, Gota Kula, ginseng, sassafras, gentian root, yellow dock, elder flowers, alfalfa, gentian root, prickly ash, St. John's Wort, blue vervain, mandrake, evening primrose, cyani flower, saffron, sandalwood, turmeric, calamus root powder, catnip, horsetail, Irish moss, nettles, fenugreek, chickweed, sarsaparilla and the tiny mustard seed. Echinacea promotes the growth and strength of red blood corpuscles, which destroy toxic invaders. Chlorophyll is a potent blood cleanser and chemically similar to hemoglobin, and the body can easily transform it into red blood cells. Pomegranate, orange juice and asparagus root tea are also beneficial.

Our bodies produce new blood every 90 days. We don't want to build new cells with tainted blood. Depending on the length of the fast, we're left with a stronger, cleaner, and more purified bloodstream. Feelings of well-being are a direct result of a bolstered immune system, and a healthy immune system is the best defense in preventing sickness and disease in the future. How clean the blood is today helps determine how we handle the healing crisis of tomorrow.

AIDS poses a most vicious problem. The HIV virus, upon entering the bloodstream, takes on the characteristic of the blood's army, the white blood cell's helper T-cells, which direct and protect the immune system. Like a wolf in sheep's clothing, the insidious AIDS virus takes on the appearance of healthy blood corpuscles. When camouflaged, the watchdogs in the blood, the billions of white blood corpuscles, don't recognize the enemy, and allow them through. Once the HIV virus multiplies, the immune system is compromised. 90% of infected people eventually die from secondary infections that would normally be no problem to a healthy immune system. When the blood is compromised, death will follow. Death isn't caused by the virus itself, but the breakdown of the blood's ability to fight. Infected people die from one of countless diseases that the blood would normally have handled with ease.

If we consider Christianity, it's interesting to consider the medium Jesus used for salvation. It's His blood! And scripture tell us His blood had no sin. Jesus' blood was pure!

> *"Forasmuch as you know that you were not redeemed with corruptible things as silver and gold, from your vain conversation received by tradition from your father: But with the precious blood of Christ without blemish and without spot." (I Peter 1:18-19)*

> *"And almost all things are by law purged with blood; and without shedding of blood is no remission." (Hebrews 9:22)*

# Fasting and the Tongue

*"The tongue of the wise promotes health."*
*(Proverbs 12:18)*

The tongue, an organ of taste and speech, is like a mirror that speaks more than words. If it's pale, it can mean anemia. A yellow tongue could signify excess bile or a liver disorder. A blue tongue is associated with the heart. As with the eyes, fingernails and bottoms of our feet, parts of the tongue are associated with different parts of the body, and inspecting it reveals what's happening within the body. A bona-fide expert should be sought for any such consultations.

A thirty-foot alimentary canal runs through our bodies from the tongue to the anus. Within this tube passes all the food we eat. Often during a fast, the tongue will become thickly coated with a slimy, toxic, white film. This can mean that the intestines are clogged, but also that the fast is loosening and removing toxins. The tongue can be scraped as needed and during a fast this process may have to be repeated often as toxins are released.

*Keep your tongue from evil." (Psalm 35:13)*

The tongue has a voracious appetite and is susceptible to today's food giants and the chemical tastes they've engineered.

Subtle and not so subtle commercials bombard us with the idea that we can eat processed and chemical garbage and be happy and sexy. These commercials and the greed behind them work well because the tongue is a difficult bodily member to control.

> *"Look also at ships: although they are so large and are driven by fierce winds, they are turned by a very small rudder wherever the pilot desires. Even so, the tongue is a little member and boasts great things. See how great a forest fire a little fire kindles! And the tongue is a fire, a world of iniquity. The tongue is so set among our members that it defiles the whole body, and sets on fire the course of nature and is set on fire by hell.... But no man can tame the tongue. It is an unruly evil, full of deadly poison." (James 3:4-8)*

When a person fasts, the gap between the appetites of the tongue and God is bridged. A fast can clear the way to God's will, and God can then help us subdue the tongue and help us to the kind of self-control that leads to abundant life. Fasting moves beyond our desire for food and drink. Fasting subdues and humbles the tongue, providing an increase in self-control. Fasting purifies this small, unruly member that can get us in so much trouble. The tongue has the power to create or destroy.

> *"If anyone among you thinks he is religious, and does not bridle his tongue but deceives his own heart, this one's religion is useless." (James 1:26)*

# Fasting and the Skin

S kin, sometimes called the third kidney, is the largest elimination organ in the body. Skin is a thin covering guarding our
outer perimeter and our first line of defense. Without this covering
we would die. One third of our blood supply is found in the blood
vessels just under the skin. Skin also ingests toxins from the air. For
every square centimeter of skin there are up to 120 sweat glands
and 200 nerve sensors. Each cell in the skin has an opening, an
escape hatch for poisons and excess, and through the glands and
blood capillaries, an infinitesimal amount of poison may surface to
cause skin eruptions, wrinkles and dozens of other problems.
People develop acne and rashes as the blood drops off toxins.

Skin consists of over 20 layers of cells. To the trained eye, each
layer can be an expression of one's health, and can become the
eventual home to toxins that accumulate in our systems. During a
fast a person can take an occasional steam bath or sauna to open the
pores. A hot bath using ginger, Epsom salts, cayenne, sage, or
baking soda can be used to induce perspiration and clean skin. It's
extremely beneficial to care for skin, especially during a fast when
toxins are released and eliminated at a greater rate. DDT, arsenic
and other volatile poisons may be expelled through the skin; often
causing permanent blotches.

Stimulating skin with a brush is extremely beneficial as it brings
more circulation to the area. Brushing helps carry off impurities and

remove dead skin. A person should not brush skin if they have open sores or skin problems. A person should always brush towards the heart, wrist to elbow, elbow to shoulders, ankles to knees, and knees to hips. Skin massage can do a world of good to internal organs and what are called disorder zones.

In moderation and correctly used, Doctor Sunshine is also recommended for skin. Sun bathing should be practiced gradually and the skin should never be burned. The sun is much more potent around water and snow, as its reflective capacity is greatly increased. Let common sense prevail! Use only natural oils to keep skin from drying.

It has been recently reported by the FDA that the PABA in most sun screens, 14 out of 17 to be exact, can be carcinogenic and can actually stimulate the growth of cancer cells. It's ironic that what the industry sells as a so-called protection against mother natures' UV rays can actually harm us. They've decided to sell us on the concept that the sun, one of our greatest nutrients, is harmful? The sun is only fire and has been so since the beginning of time. All of the sudden there's a wave of hysterical fear, and we're not to be in the sun? And if we do go into the sun, we need to buy their product? Wow! All we need to do is go to Pacific Islands or Equatorial regions and see people exposed to the sun all day long, every day and they rarely get skin cancer. DON'T BUY THE LIE! Sunscreen is big business. Use natural oils and acclimate the skin gradually.

When sunshine is absorbed by skin it sets off a series of events that produce vitamin D, a necessary non-toxic ingredient for absorption of calcium, phosphorus, and other minerals. If the body does not get enough sun, bones and the growth process suffers, causing rickets in children and osteomalacia in adults. True vitamin D is produced by ultraviolet rays, not so-called vitamin D synthesized in the laboratory, which is toxic in large doses, and serves only to relieve you of your money and create more expensive urine. UV rays help lower blood pressure, increase heart efficiency, benefit sex hormones, reduce cholesterol, assist in treatment of psoriasis and kill bacteria.

Many skin problems can result from nothing more than a poor diet. To have healthy skin, we must protect our inner organs from harmful chemicals. Ingesting chemicals will eventually put pressure on the skin. We must protect our outer layer from many profit based dangers and industries. Many commercial soaps and shampoos should be avoided, because they contain synthetic and harmful ingredients. Read the labels or go to a health food store.

When caring for skin, some commercial cosmetics and perfumes should also be avoided. Some of them are concocted only for greed and to cloak imperfections, not for health. Skin must breathe, and these products plug pores. Most contain products that are not only detrimental to the skin, but when absorbed can cause numerous other problems. Only biologically natural products should be used. Nature makes many oils and natural creams that help skin. Aloe Vera, St. John's Wort oil and similar natural creams and oils are extremely beneficial for the care and protection of skin. Aloe Vera is even good on burns. When we care for our outer skin layer we care for nerves, cells and blood vessels just underneath the surface. Beneficial herbs are chickweed, balm of Gilead, red clover and calendula.

Water therapy can enhance and support the healing process and influence skin and inner organs. Hydrotherapy, steam baths, and whirlpools soften the skin and open pores, causing perspiration and giving toxins a quick and safe exit route. Herbs that induce perspiration are: catnip, cayenne, ginger, peppermint, elder flowers, yarrow flowers and lemon. Any herb that promotes circulation and heats the system will help open pores. Skin softeners include sesame, flaxseed, olive, and almond oil, and herbs such as comfrey, chickweed and slippery elm. Salt is a great remedy for skin. Bathing in the ocean is recommended for edema, swellings, glandular and thyroid problems. Gargling with salt water is good for the inner linings of the mouth and acts as a disinfectant.

# Fasting and the Colon

The colon, which includes the rectum, is an efficient sewage system, but by neglect, overeating and abuse it becomes a stagnant cesspool. Colon walls can become encrusted with hard, fecal matter. Such a condition hampers absorption of vital nutrients and creates a breeding ground for problems. When the colon is clean, our system is healthy and efficient, but let it stagnate, and it'll dispatch the poisons of decay, fermentation and putrefaction into our bloodstream and throughout the body.

The colon is approximately 5 feet long and 2 1/2 inches wide. A neglected or overloaded colon can poison the brain and nervous system causing irritability and even depression. It can poison and weaken the heart, poison the lungs so breath is foul, poison the digestive organs so we're distressed and bloated, and poison the blood that in turn leads to sallow and unhealthy skin. An unkempt colon can poison every organ and part of the body, age us prematurely and cause stiffness and pain in our joints. By neglecting the colon we can develop neuritis, dull yellow eyes and a sluggish brain. Under such conditions, the pleasure of life is gone.

Signs that a body has an unhealthy intestinal tract are headaches, depression, tension, coated tongue, insomnia, gas, weight increase, bloating, skin problems, menstrual problems and fatigue. Other colon problems are constipation and diarrhea. These problems are most often treated with over the counter remedies, but such man-made remedies neglect to heal the cause. Another problem is colon-stasis, which is lack of bowel movement. This can result from stress, unresolved emotional problems, anger and pain, a bad diet, or from not eating enough roughage. The colon backs up and toxins become trapped. Constipation means that toxins are fermenting and decaying in the colon, often being reabsorbed into the bloodstream.

The colon is affected by the food we eat. Putrefaction or abnormal bacteria can result from eating refined carbohydrates such as white flour, sugar or stale foods as a steady diet. In areas where people live off the land and eat natural food, such conditions are almost non-existent. Additional studies show that when these same people are integrated into our society, they develop the same problems we have.

Constipation is serious, as hard stools accumulate and are reabsorbed with water back into the system. The putrefied stool enters the bloodstream and travels throughout the body, including the brain, which causes headaches or more serious maladies. When this happens, our system literally lives in its own waste. When the colon backs up and overloads the body, most people in Western society continue to eat three square meals a day and take some over the counter remedy to mask the symptoms. Also, when stool backs up, the colon stretches and small pockets called "diverticuli" develop. Strain in elimination causes hemorrhoids (piles) and varicosities (varicose veins) which are caused by the restricted flow of blood to and from the heart. Phlebitis can also occur, which is an inflammation of the vein, and can be fatal.

Waste material moves through the colon more readily when stools are soft, usually a day to a day and a half after we've eaten. In today's society, with our processed and heavy unnatural diets, it often takes an average of 3 to 4 days for that particular meal to be eliminated. This puts extra stress on the body, makes us feel sluggish, takes our energy away, and adds to depression. How many people suffer needlessly? How many suffer due to lack of knowledge?

A number of doctors in our culture performed and documented over twenty thousand operations and found few healthy colons. When the body gets too full of toxins, the body becomes overloaded and the toxins interfere with proper nutrition and cell rebuilding. A healthy colon should evacuate once for every meal eaten, otherwise there's a buildup of putrefying material and we're not at peak efficiency. Such unhealthy conditions speak volumes for the dramatic increase of diseases like cancer and the endless complaints regarding lack of energy.

When we eat and drink the colon absorbs liquid in the small intestine and moves solids on to be eliminated with a wavelike motion called peristalsis. During a fast this process subsides almost completely, so waste material that's left in the colon remains. It's a good idea to take herbal laxative products the day before a fast, as they neutralize toxins and fermentation in the colon before fasting, passing them harmlessly through the body.

Fasting is the best treatment for bowel toxicity. Fasting will strengthen and clean a colon, but proper elimination is mostly dependent on a good diet. Certain herbs, like cascara bark, senna and rhubarb root help create lubricants to move stool. Psyllium husk, which is the base for most colon cleansers, turns into a soft gel and will collect a lot of refuse for elimination. Marshmallow, Aloe Vera and slippery elm are also beneficial lubricants.

Inside diverticuli pockets, toxic accumulations may remain for a lifetime. Organic matter makes its way into these pockets and putrefies; the poison can then be released into the body and picked up by the blood. The blood takes the poison and deposits it in the next weakest organ, thereby causing numerous symptoms and diseases. Since everyone has a different chemical makeup and different strengths and weaknesses, the symptoms vary from individual to individual, and are the reason so many people suffering from misdiagnosed ailments, or the doctor often finds no problem at all. How many people feeling tired or sluggish, or unduly weak have been told it's all in their head? Perhaps they should also check their colon. Perhaps they should fast and clean the waste out of their bodies.

During a fast we can also help remove stool from our bowels by use of enemas and colonics. As in water or juice fasting, there are also many differing schools of thought concerning these artificial cleansing techniques. Some doctors encourage their use, while others encourage a more natural approach. Nonetheless, if a person chooses to clean their colon using colonics or enemas, they should never overdue it. We mentioned that the body eliminates by muscle contractions called peristalsis. Enemas and colonics should not be used often, for the natural muscles will atrophy, like any other muscle of the body that is not used.

The pro enema/colonic group believes that during the first few days of a fast, a little help can be beneficial to eliminate what's left in the colon after the muscle motion subsides. During fasting there's a decrease of evacuation and all putrefied material and toxins remain in the fecal matter. Also, bile accumulates from deposits of residue in the intestines and can't be excreted when no food is eaten. When all other impurities are burned by autolysis, the artificial cleansing proponents like the idea of assisting elimination from the alimentary canal, thereby rinsing the colon and further easing pressure on the entire system.

A colonic will use up to 5 gallons of water verses up to 2 quarts for an enema. Used sparingly, both are useful and helpful for personal hygiene. Both produce immediate effects of lightness and cleanliness. Waste products are eliminated so they won't be reabsorbed. Enema bags can be purchased at any drug store. There are bottles available that are already filled with water and other bags you can fill by yourself. Any added chemicals should be avoided. Colonics should be administered in a clean environment and by reputable professional practitioners. Colonics are more effective, use more water, and may even remove refuse from diverticuli pockets. Certain gentle herbs can be beneficial and added to the water.

Enemas assist the body in cleansing and detoxifying by washing out the entire lower colon only. Professor Ehret, whose longest fast was 49 days, estimated that: *"The average person has as much as 10 pounds of uneliminated feces in their bowels, continuously poisoning her/his bloodstream and the entire system."* Enemas can be taken at least once, preferably twice a day upon rising and before going to bed. One pint to one quart of lukewarm distilled water is sufficient.

Enemas are far from being a spiritual experience, yet they can have a beneficial role in fasting. The thought of inserting a liter of water into the intestine to flush out waste may seem beyond consideration. But the quickest and most efficient way of removing toxic waste from the intestines is an enema. The lymph glands, which line the intestinal wall, absorb and filter fluid from the feces. Flushing water through the colon causes a healing reflex. Lukewarm water cleanses the lymph glands attached to the colon, and waste is washed from the system. If you're not comfortable doing an enema, psyllium husk or flaxseeds are a good alternative, as is an herbal colon cleanse formula.

While administering an enema, it's beneficial to lie on one side, and then on the other side to promote the water to fill the lower intestines to maximum effectiveness. Catnip, sesame oil, yellow dock, bayberry bark, raspberry, comfrey, castor oil or honey may be added to the water for various positive effects such as preventing irritation. Psyllium seeds and mullein are helpful in the treatment of diverticulosis.

Herbs like psyllium seeds, chia seeds, and flax seeds, when mixed with large amounts of water, will absorb up to 15 times their weight in water. The bulk will expand and move through the colon taking almost everything in its path with it. The bulk will fill many of the pockets of diverticuli, thereby removing hard to clean areas. It's important when using these natural laxatives to drink as much water as possible to avoid the hardening of these herbs in the colon. A person may feel a bit bloated, but the process is extremely beneficial. Drug store varieties should be scrutinized to see what is added to the herbs, such as massive amounts of sugar.

I have personally used enemas, colonics and colon cleansers, and at other times just left things to nature. All my fasts have been beneficial. Personally I prefer pure fire, pure water, pure air, and pure Spirit, and everything as natural as possible. I don't require scientific verification for everything, but I trust God's nature and God's principles. I feel that a person can employ any of these methods and they will receive great benefits. Pick the method you're most comfortable with, just fast.

# Fasting, the Liver and the Gallbladder

The word liver comes from the word for living. No one can sustain a healthy body unless the liver is clean and functioning properly. Of all detoxifying organs the liver is the most important. Besides being the body's filter, the liver also stores glucose. Excluding the skin, it's the largest organ and also the most abused. Overly processed foods, chemicals, tobacco, alcohol and drugs have a devastating effect on the liver, which processes 3 pints of blood a minute. The liver neutralizes and eliminates what it can, the rest it stores. There are cases where people have 10 to 20 lbs. of rubbish stored in the liver.

The liver acts like a buffer zone for our bodies. It regulates blood sugar, but like any other part of the body, it can only handle so much. Once the liver is overwhelmed with toxins, it can no longer keep the body clean and the poisons will overflow, accumulate somewhere else and a chronic disease may develop. The liver can take a lot of abuse. It'll send out no alarm signals until considerable damage has been done. Some naturalistic practitioners are expert in determining an ailing liver by analyzing eyes, hair or skin texture. Fasting is the fountain of youth for the liver!

Because most accumulated poisons are inorganic and artificial in nature, the body is ill equipped to deal with them. We're made of natural elements and the body is normally only able to deal with and recognize natural elements. Inorganic and chemical elements that are not recognized and dealt with can damage the sensitive and delicate organs of the body. The liver, along with the lungs, kidneys, and colon catch and store such particles and often suffer the most. The liver is particularly vulnerable because of its rich blood supply and its attempts to protect the rest of the body by absorbing the harmful materials. The liver even attempts to absorb stress and anxiety.

A person with a toxic liver can exhibit many symptoms such as headaches, including migraines, heartburn, gas, menstrual irregularities, bodily pain, tired burning feet, back pain and emotional breakdowns like depression. A person with a toxic liver may develop an aversion to fried foods and acids like orange juice. When this happens, itching sensations can occur all over the body.

Our own bodies produce toxins, but generally the liver becomes toxic due to abuse. It's bombarded continually by free radicals and pollutants. If the liver, dealing with thousands of various chemicals is badly degenerated, cleansing must be done in stages. Start with short juice fasts. Avoid heavy proteins, refined flours and fatty foods. Eat meals of fruits or vegetables between the fasts. If a person suspects a seriously overloaded, toxic liver, it's wise to begin detoxifying the liver before beginning a serious fast, so that the blood stream isn't inundated with the accumulated poisons during the first few days.

There are many herbs that help detoxify the liver, such as dandelion root, gentian, golden seal root, red beet root, fringe tree, yellow dock, centaury, rosemary, Oregon grape root, watermelon seeds, bayberry, boldo, pan pien lien, artichoke leaves, blessed thistle and ginger. To rebuild and tone the liver take Oregon grape root, wild yam root, dandelion root and ginger.

Gallstones usually form from bad diet, especially cholesterol. Bitter herbs can often dissolve gallstones. Dandelion, Culver's root, Oregon grape, balm of Gilead, bitterroot, wild yam, greater celendine and wahoo work well. It's also beneficial to take a tablespoon of olive oil mixed with lemon juice every hour.

A novice faster would be well-advised to detoxify before starting a fast regardless of their own perception of health. Begin by drinking distilled water with one fresh lemon everyday for at least a week (unless kidneys are overly toxic). This will help flush the liver. Of course, it should go without saying that a person should not put anything harmful into the body during this time. Apple cider vinegar is also beneficial. In serious cases, a castor oil pack can be applied to the outside of the liver as often as feasible. Another remedial measure has a person grind one organic lemon in a blender, add a tablespoon of pure olive oil, put the mixture through a strainer, add distilled water and take daily for a week or two.

# Fasting and the Kidneys

The kidneys are two important organs on each side of the small of the back. Their function is to eliminate liquids and control chemical content. Kidneys also help purify the bloodstream. Kidneys filter blood, regulate acid and alkali levels, expel about three pints of waste a day, and send 98% of liquids back to be reabsorbed into the system.

Kidneys, which are made of a million tiny filters called nephrons, seldom rest even during a fast. During a fast we should drink a lot of liquid as the kidneys stay busy flushing toxins. A distilled-water fast helps flush kidneys and they get some relief, as distilled water contains no minerals. It takes 2 or 3 days into a fast for serious detoxification to start, but once it does, the blood stream becomes loaded with poison excreted from cells for disposal through the kidneys.

Diuretic herbs help cleanse and increase urine, such as parsley, agrimony, broom, cornsilk, couchgrass and horsetail. Goldenrod tea can stimulate and activate the kidneys. Elder flowers, pan pien lien, peppermint, juniper berries, golden seal root, cubeb berries, watermelon seeds, buchu leaves, shavegrass, red beet root, marshmallow, uva ursi, ginger and lovage also stimulate the kidneys and bladder while they promote perspiration.

Fasting can irritate damaged kidneys due to the amount of toxins they filter. Try short juice fasts of 3 to 5 days before progressing to longer fasts. Avoid high-protein meals, refined flours, sugars, commercial hydrogenated oils and fats.

# Fasting and the Lungs

The Amazon Rain Forest is the lungs of planet earth, as air generates when sunshine absorbs into its abundance of green leaves. Plants convert water and carbon dioxide into a carbohydrate, which releases oxygen into the air creating the energy we need to live. Our respiratory system takes oxygen from the air and needs a constant supply to burn carbohydrates for cells to maintain life. Oxygen is moved about the body by the respiratory and circulatory systems.

We can go without food or even water for a while, but we can't live without air for more than a few minutes. Breathing is the first thing we do when we are born. Breathing sustains us, and our last gasp of air is the last thing we do before we die. Lungs are also one of the greatest receptacles of toxins and chemicals. In cities we breathe in pollutants every day. In some cities, they post warnings that people should stay indoors because of poor air quality. Some people go even further and pollute their own lungs. Smoking is the worst thing we can do to our lungs.

Lungs need fresh air, and exercise is one of the best ways to energize them. Lungs are comprised of millions of tiny air sacs and enveloped by networks of blood vessels that can't store the oxygen, but only move it. Blood also brings toxins to the lungs, which are then expelled when we breathe. This is the greatest benefit of forcing large amount of oxygen in and out of the body during exercise. Deep breathing exercises are also beneficial for endurance, stamina, and reduction of stress. All diseases detest high levels of oxygenation.

Lungs are muscles in the form of expanding and depressing bellows. A stressed lung will fill with mucous to protect itself. Expectorant herbs help expel mucous. Elecampane, white horehound and bloodroot cause us to cough. Other expectorants are garlic, mullein, fennel seed and lobelia. Mullein, chickweed, pan pien lien, slippery elm and coltsfoot soothe and relax the bronchial system.

# Fasting and Weight Loss

*"Everything in excess is opposed to nature."*
*Hippocrates*

Why are so many people in our society overweight? A recent survey stated that 6 out of 10 people would like to lose weight. There may be deep environmental, spiritual or psychological reasons for our obesity, but also heredity, glandular malfunction, chemical imbalances and just plain overeating. Regardless of the root cause, excess weight puts undue pressure on every part of the body.

*"A full stomach does not like to think."*
*Old German Proverb*

Eating too much, especially excessive protein creates acidity, and the more acid we produce the more sluggish we become. Once energy is diverted to handle excess food, the body and mind are robbed of much of their natural vigor. 300,000 people a year die in the US from obesity. According to the AMA, 58 million or 35% are considered obese, over 75% are at least ten pounds overweight. Experts consider a person weighing 20% more than normal weight to be clinically obese. It's estimated that over 80 million people are overweight in America alone. The US Congressional Nutrition

Monitoring Committee reported that up to 80% of Americans from ages 25 to 74 are considered overweight. There's no good function for excess fat.

> *"The continually stuffed body cannot see secret things." Primitive Amazulu*

The *Center for Disease Control* in Atlanta says obesity increased 10% in the 1980's, and another 5% in the 1990's. They talk in terms of epidemic proportions. How many people suffer needlessly? How many suffer from high blood pressure, heart attacks, diabetes, breathing difficulties or skin problems? The associated emotional problems and low self-esteem can't be calculated.

Over the last decade, the health movement has severely backfired. It's been proven diets don't work. During the 80's the health spa business boomed. Jogging and bicycle trails were packed, but in actuality health consciousness has all but plumbed out. Exercise machines have been abandoned and lie dormant in garages and basements. Many children eat nothing but junk food, with no discipline whatsoever. Statistics for the next generation are appalling. Their lack of discipline will lead to obesity, a buildup of toxins, poor elimination and an overly acid condition.

Food is the first thing we crave at birth and our appetite is our strongest and most basic desire. Eating is natural, but our society eats too much. Hungry or not, its three square meals a day, like gospel. The organs receive, hold, move, digest, process and eliminate more food than needed, and people complain about lack of energy. Obesity is the greatest common denominator to most disease, and the greatest reason for inactivity and physical unfitness that imperils us. It's the greatest cause of a shortened life.

In December of 2001, U.S. Surgeon General David Satcher warned that; *"Obesity is reaching epidemic proportions in America, and could soon cause as much preventable disease and death as cigarette smoking. More than 61% of U.S. adults and 13% of adolescents currently meet the scientific definition of obesity, and some 300,000 Americans die each year from health problems directly related to obesity," he noted, adding "this is probably the most sedentary generation of people in the history of the world! This is not about aesthetics and it's not about appearances,"* Satcher said. *"We're talking about health!"* Satcher estimates that twelve hundred Americans die daily from weight-related illnesses, with rates of overweight and obesity rising across all age, ethnic, geographic and socioeconomic groups. Will this warning be heeded? In 1996, when just over 50% of the population was considered obese, the warning went unheeded and statistics are on the rise.

> *"We live off of 25% of what we eat. The doctors live off the other 75%" Benjamin Franklin*

What has the food industry done to help besides invent the drive through window? There are ten thousand food ads on television every year. If these were healthy foods, it wouldn't be so bad, but we're talking quick fix sugar cereals, candy, beer, and soda. Even the portions of many of our products, especially in the ever-growing fast food industry, have increased significantly. We eat quarter pounders, double quarter pounders, triple quarter pounders and triple quarter pounders with bacon. French fries have gone from large and king size to off the map *biggie* fries. Candy bars have tripled in size, and the sodas are so large it takes two hands just to carry them. Car manufacturers have had to reinvent the cup holder to hold these sodas. One helping of ice cream has the fat of a half a stick of butter. Did you ever try to find something healthy in a convenience store?

> *"Many dishes, many diseases" Benjamin Franklin*

Family is in decline, unemployment and violence are on the rise, recessions loom. People are lonely, isolated and alienated. We're doing less and less manual labor. We ride elevators, escalators and use computers. We're glued to machines, and we don't even dial phones anymore. And what do we do as a society to sublimate the frustration? We eat. It's the most basic gratification available.

*"Eat to live, not live to eat." Benjamin Franklin*

An article in Time magazine sought an anti-flab formula, the great hope of mankind. Diet pills and drugs that block our normal biological triggers have become a billion-dollar industry. Liposuction and cosmetic surgeries are available everywhere. For the love of money, doctor drug dealer is selling us billions of dollars of mostly worthless pills and empty promises. The food industry will peddle anything that sells. We continue to buy illusions, and we stuff the empty holes in our hearts with unnatural food that doesn't fit.

Being overweight is sometimes no more than a problem of eating the right foods. We need to eat. We should enjoy eating, but inefficient nutrition can lead to obesity. The body needs foods it can process. Weight gain is often symptomatic of a poor diet, and inefficiencies of conversion, absorption and elimination. Inefficiency leads to fatigue which in turn leads a person to reach for a candy bar, donut, soda, or cup of coffee, and the vicious cycle continues. The body gets a quick surge, but as soon as the quick fix wears off, the person is fatigued again.

Just because people eat natural food doesn't necessarily mean they'll be fit. Some of these so-called healthy eaters still combine foods improperly, overeat, eat erratically and ignore proper protein balance. Most people intent on health will stop smoking, drinking, give up coffee and drugs, but change eating habits? Never! And talk about getting pulled in two directions at once. The media sells slim, while the food industry sells the over processed and denatured food that makes us sick and fat. People binge and purge. We have the phenomenon of bulimia, and anorexia. Society is fast becoming more and more dysfunctional in their habits.

Many people overeat simply because they're starving. Their body is so caked with poison and unnatural matter from the tongue to the rectum that they can no longer properly absorb nutrients and vitamins. Organs and systems no longer send nutrients to other parts of their body. A simple cleansing of the body, and they can begin to receive nutrients they need. This poisoned, packed system may be a breeding ground for parasites and worms, which in turn also feed on the nutrients that are needed by the body.

Fasting has no peer in weight loss. During a fast a person loses weight immediately. A normal person averages about a pound of weight loss a day, though obese people have averaged up to 2.5 pounds a day over the first couple of weeks. The weight loss is more dramatic during the beginning, because of water loss and the elimination of salt. As metabolism slows down, weight loss is less dramatic. If a person fasts just to lose weight, three to seven day fasts are adequate, and the fasts should be supported by good diet and exercise.

The following herbs can be combined to promote weight loss by suppressing the appetite. They also strengthen the immune system. Dandelion, fennel, black walnut, chickweed, licorice root, gotu kola, saffron, kelp, cascara sagrada, red clover, Echinacea, hawthorn berries and papaya.

# How to Break a Fast

*"Even a fool can fast, but only a wise man knows how to break a fast properly and to build up properly after the fast." Dr. Otto Buchinger*

In (*Matthew 4:2*) we learn that after forty days, Jesus hungered. He broke His fast and ate. The word breakfast literally means to break a fast. A fast can be ended at any time, but a long fast should end when autolysis has completed burning away all nonessential material and true hunger returns. Physically speaking, breaking the fast is the most important part of a fast. It's imperative a person come off a fast gradually to avoid digestive trauma and undoing the benefits that were gained. This is where real will power is needed, often more than for the fast itself.

Always break a fast gently with high quality, fresh organic foods that are minimally processed. This is essential to maximize the benefits of the fast. After fasting, your body is like a sponge awaiting nutrients. You'll need high quality materials to build high quality cell structure. The longer the fast, the more care should be taken in breaking it. When a person is ready to eat, they'll awaken a hungry giant. Food will taste so, so good.

Upton Sinclair, a turn of the century health advocate, wrote this concerning his fasting experiences: *"The perspiration and breath become offensive; the tongue becomes heavily coated, so that you*

135

*can scrape the material off with a knife.... And this will go on for ten days, for twenty days, and in some cases for as long as forty or fifty days and then suddenly a strange thing occurs...the symptoms all come to an end. The tongue clears, the breath becomes sweet, and the appetite suddenly awakens. During the period of the fast you lose all interest in food. You almost forget there is such a thing as eating: you can look at food without any more desire for it than you have to swallow marbles or carpet tacks. But then suddenly, appetite returns, as I have explained, you can think of nothing but food."*

There should be a profound sense of accomplishment and well-being at the end of the fast. We must be aware of certain changes that have taken place. The stomach and over thirty feet of intestinal tract have shrunk. The metabolism has been slowed to nil and the digestive system has also shut down and must be awakened slowly. Too much food put into this slowed system will overload it and cause severe discomfort. A person wouldn't rev up an engine to a high rate of rpm's in neutral and then drop it into drive. There's no need to shock the system here, but reenter the process gently, smoothly, and with common sense.

The typical Western diet of junk food should be avoided altogether. Many health benefits can be undone during these first few days if one overeats. Caution, discipline, patience, and above all, common sense are needed! The fast should be broken with a gradual and sensible transition. A safe rule of thumb is to build back up into a normal metabolism, using the number of days a person has fasted. In other words, if a person fasted seven days, they would slowly work back into a normal diet for seven days. During this reentry phase, a lot more healing, rejuvenation and detoxification can take place as the body is now clean and functioning more efficiently.

Great care should be taken to eat slowly, and not eat rich, processed foods. Gorging with food after a long fast can put too much stress on the heart. Only the finest ingredients should be put into the body after the fast and thereafter. A person should eat soft, high water content foods that are easily digested, such as light broth soups or small salads. A person can seek food from a garden or organically labeled food from a health food store. Nothing that's hard to digest should be eaten. Melons and fruits such as grapefruit, oranges, apples, grapes, pears, tomatoes, and mangoes are the easiest to digest. After a fast, it's imperative to begin a diet that's closer to our physiological makeup, namely natural foods.

After a fast, taste buds naturally gravitate towards cleaner, healthier foods like fruits, vegetables, grains, seeds and nuts.

The toxic memory is greatly reduced, so this period provides an excellent opportunity to reorganize and change eating patterns. If a person breaks a lengthy water fast, it's recommended a person do juices and broth in the transition before eating anything solid again. A person should not eat too much and should eat things easily digestible.

Restarting the digestive system to normal performance can take a day, or it can take over a week depending on the particular person's metabolism and the length of the fast. Over-exaggerate! Sip, nibble and chew every bite! Eat small amounts and spread your meals out. Many small meals are better than a few large ones. Digestive glands can be stimulated with herbs like cinnamon, peppermint, star anise, licorice, ginger, caraway, cardamom, fennel or cloves.

### Fruits that can be eaten during the first days after a significant fast

| | | |
|---|---|---|
| Watermelon | Papaya | Grapes |
| Melons | Pineapple | Mango |
| Oranges | Apples | Peaches |
| Cantaloupe | Grapefruit | Kiwi |
| Tangerines | Limes | Berries |
| Plums | | |

Fruit and broth are excellent on day one. Small additions of vegetables can be added on successive days. Smoothies are a wonderful meal after the first couple of days. They can be made with fruit and a small portion of bananas, brewer's yeast, seeds, herbs and yogurt. Lightly steamed veggies in their broth with whole grain brown rice can be added gradually after a few days, and used as part of your maintenance diet. Combine common sense with imagination. Natural foods are nutritional and free from additives. Eat foods that have ingredients necessary to sustain a healthy life. Fruits and vegetables, especially green foods, are full of phytonutrients, vitamins, antioxidants, enzymes and minerals, and help prevent disease.

> *"Therefore, whether you eat or drink, or whatever you do, do all to the glory of God." (I Corinthians 10:31)*

# Diet and Nutrition

*"The doctor of the future will give no medicine but will interest his patients in the care of the human frame, in diet, and in the cause and prevention of disease." Benjamin Franklin*

Far too many people in our western culture go hungry. Oh, they put enough food into their mouths and get enough calories, but their bodies aren't fully nourished. They're actually malnourished, while being over fed. The consumer eats devitalized foods, and because of toxic overload and a myriad of other bodily malfunctions, can't fully absorb and utilize the nutrients they ate. If we put defective gas and oil into an engine, it won't run well, if at all. If we continue to put incompatible elements into the engine, we'll more than likely ruin it altogether.

*"To fare well implies partaking of food as do not disagree with body or mind." Socrates*

Health experts have compiled statistics claiming that two out of three people die from diseases that start from diets lacking the necessary nutrients for health. They say only 20% of our illnesses are caused by bacteria and other poisons. Over 60 million people go on diets every year and almost all of them gain back weight because they're malnourished. The body instinctually knows what it needs, and when it does not receive proper nutrition, it sends more hunger signals, which must be satisfied. People fulfill these hunger signals, and as they continue to eat non-nutritious foods, the body picks out only what it can use. What the body can't use, digest and eliminate, it stores in fat cells. And sadly, statistics maintain that approximately 70% of US adults are overweight.

If we eat chemically refined, so-called processed, enriched, gassed, treated, artificially preserved and flavored foods packed with additives, dyes and waxes our body will not run well. Food is prepared in this manner, not because it's good for us, but because it's good for business. It's about the love of money. The profiteers strip food of nutrient rich natural elements and replace it with all kinds of harmful additives to make the food look attractive and to create a longer shelf life. Even with so many facts staring us in the face, we continue to eat the garbage and support these profiteers.

> *"Life is a selection, nothing more."*
> *Ralph Waldo Emerson*

Human bodies are chemical factories. Every cell is composed of the same elements as the universe about us, namely water, fire, earth and air. Water manifests as saliva, digestive juices, mucous, urine and blood. Inner fire, like the sun, heats our bodies, digests food, and controls our metabolic rates and enzyme systems. Earth is the solid substance upon which all the other elements cling and revolve namely muscle, tissue, skin, bones, hair, nails, tendons and cartilage. There's also air within the body, which we inhale and exhale continually through our lungs. Air also moves in our bodies in the form of gas. When a scientist examines cells under a microscope, he finds they too are moved about by gas, like tiny planets within a universe unseen and undetected by our senses. When the body dies, the elements disperse back into nature and return to their natural state. It stands to reason that we should eat naturally, as like feeds like. We don't put olive oil into the gas tank of our car, because the car is made to run on gasoline. Similarly, the body is made to run on natural elements and not man-made chemicals and unnatural composites. It's hard to build or maintain a healthy body while we continue to eat unnatural foods.

Many of us have been exposed to the immortalized words of George Bernard Shaw, *"You are what you eat"*. Mr. Shaw also said, *"Show me what a person eats and I'll show you what they are."*

Studies on primitive societies show they don't suffer from some of our common diseases such as arthritis, cancer, or rheumatism. It was also noted that these peoples on average ate one third to one half less than we do. They also don't eat processed foods like white flour or refined sugars and other low value carbohydrates. It has been noted that whenever civilization encroached upon these cultures, their traditional natural diets were replaced by processed foods and their incidence of disease increased.

We can view the body as a microcosm (small universe), and the world about us as a macrocosm (large universe). Except for size, our bodies and the universe are made of relatively the same essential elements. If we desire to improve our lives on a physical level, to stay healthy, to clean our bodies, it's imperative we evaluate, and if necessary, change our diets. Everyone's microcosm is different and each diet should be evaluated according to each person's disposition. A person needs to consider whether the food is hot, sweet, pungent, salty, oily, dry, bitter or astringent. All these foods will have unique effects. Seasons of the year and climate are other determining factors in choosing diet. Most determinations are common sense. If a person suffers from cold, it makes perfect sense to eat hot foods like peppers, cayenne, and garlic to dry mucous and warm and balance the body. Conversely, a person with a cold should not eat ice cream, milk or other mucous forming foods. The quality and freshness of food is also important. A person also shouldn't eat when they're not hungry and should never overeat.

> *"Dine with little, sup with less, do better still: sleep supperless. To lengthen thy life, lessen thy meals."*
> *Ben Franklin*

If a person suffers from indigestion they should fast and not compound the problem with more food. If a body is already over-loaded and can't handle what it already has in it, how will it handle additional food? The body must produce more bile and enzymes to handle the overload and the body can't continually meet such demands. Again, common sense is indispensable.

We can't expect to be successful with fasting, detoxification, and herbal therapy if we don't begin to eat natural, nutritional food. If a person gets sick, they should immediately abstain from any heavy, hard to digest foods so that available energy is immediately diverted to the sickness at hand and not to digesting more food.

> *"A good and proper diet in disease is worth a hundred medicines and no amount of medication can do good to a patient who does not observe a strict regimen of diet." Charaka Samhita*

There's absolutely no excuse for a poor diet, especially in America where food is plentiful. We put food into our own mouths. A poor diet is made up of junk food, processed, devitalized, clog-ging, stale, dead, and overcooked and fast food. Such a diet sets the stage for intestinal disorders. Junk (dead) food lacks natural living enzymes, nutrients, vitamins and minerals that are needed to help with digestion and assimilation.

Our bodies are wondrous mechanisms designed by God to process natural food. Our bodies aren't made to eat man-made profit-based foods. When we eat these foreign substances, our bodily functions have no way to recognize them, and the body loses energy dealing with them. Toxins and poison might be eliminated, but they may also get packed away into remote corners of our system and accumulate until, in its natural inclination, the body develops a cold or fever, or something far worse. If we continue the abuse, like dominoes, other parts of the body will be affected.

From the famous Bircher-Benner health clinic, started in 1897 in Zurich, Switzerland, its founder Dr. Max Bircher-Benner, a major proponent of natural foods wrote; *"We are oppressed by an overwhelming burden of incurable disease, which hangs over our lives like a dark cloud. It is a burden that will not disappear until men become aware of the basic laws of life."* Among basic laws of life are the laws of nutrition. The body functions normally when it receives live foods. Nature means that which is life-like, not artificial. Live foods lead to proper digestion, assimilation, absorption and elimination.

Experts have concluded that most modern day disease result from environmental conditions, and the most intrinsic contact we have with our environment is food. Food is also one of our greatest desires. Almost every function humans engage in revolves around food, such as banquets, wedding, funerals, birthdays, holidays, business meetings, dating, and movies. "Hey, I quit smoking, drinking and drugs, but don't touch my food." Gluttony and bad eating habits are acceptable and subtle sins in our culture. They cause a multitude of ills, and they're also one of the single most changeable factors.

> *"What was paradise, but a garden full of vegetables,*
> *and herbs, and pleasures, nothing there but delights."*
> *William Lawson*

God has put all we need to eat into the nature about us. The bottom line was well stated in 1930 by Dr. Victor G. Rocine who said; *"If we eat wrongly, no doctor can cure us. If we eat rightly, no doctor is needed."*

# Things to Avoid

*"Yet even now, says the Lord, return to me with all your heart with fasting..." (Joel 2:12)*

**W**e've all heard the saying, "ignorance is no excuse". If we put our hand in a rattlesnake hole, chances are we'll get bit whether we know it's a rattlesnake hole or not. If we know that there's a rattlesnake in the hole, we wouldn't put our hand in, would we? There are many silent snakes among us, and many rattlesnake holes that can destroy us or make our lives miserable. When we become aware of them, we should use wisdom and avoid them.

*"A prudent man foresees evil and hides himself"*
*(Proverbs 22:3)*

There are many pitfalls in what we eat. Large food companies manipulate and subvert our legal processes in order to profit heavily from their processed foods. As early as 1912 the FDA was taken over by business interests, and through manipulation and fraud, they have conned the American market and overlook and ignore health for profit.

*"Everything in excess is opposed by nature."*
*Hippocrates*

Elmer Nelson, who became the food industries' spokesperson said: *"It is wholly unscientific to state that a well-fed body is more able to resist disease than less well-fed body. My overall opinion is that there hasn't been enough experimentation to prove dietary deficiencies makes one more susceptible to disease." Washington Post, Oct. 26, 1949*

An incredible statement! All this happened as doctors from the US and Europe screamed in protest, all to no avail. There were opponents who mysteriously died and studies, books, and pertinent paperwork disappeared. Such manipulation opened the door to our denatured food programs and the food giants we're held hostage by today. The same lobby encouraged chemical farming, most of which continues today. Processed food has become so ingrained in our culture it's hardly even questioned anymore. It's the norm and totally accepted. Even the healthy person is subject to and exposed to man-made poisons and should make a lifestyle of fasting and periodic detoxification to counter this outrage.

In recent years we've seen how powerful the tobacco lobbyists are in Washington. Tobacco, a cause of up to 20% of all cancers, among other diseases, is an insidious killer. Smoking slows down our blood circulation and narrows our blood vessels and arteries. Ill effects of one cigarette harm everything in our bodies and take about a day to wear off. Even though it has been proven cigarettes are poisonous to our bodies, and that smoking kills as it destroys the quality of life, big business can't be stopped. There's too much money involved and the people getting paid are entrenched into the political system. Politicians support large companies, which in turn support their candidacy. Smoking is most damaging if a person is on a fast, as there's no other nutrient to water it down.

In our world we inadvertently ingest poisons no matter how careful we are. But there are ways we can minimize our exposure. We shouldn't be destroyed for lack of knowledge. Perhaps with knowledge, and if enough people show proactive concern, we can begin to reverse the destruction of our planet, clean the water, the air, and the soil, thereby insuring us and our children clean, natural, nutritional food and an overall healthier life.

Read labels! The FDA now requires manufacturers to list

specific information about the contents on labels. Unfortunately they do nothing about additives that have been known to cause cancer. If we continue to put poison into the body, no fasting program, cleansing process or herbal formula will help in the long run. A Surgeon General's Report in 1988 stated that up to two-thirds of all deaths in the US in 1987 were related to diets. Almost a million new cases of cancer were also reported, this in a period of significant decline of tobacco use.

Our foods are laced with disease causing substances. Mono-sodium glutamate is known to cause cancer in laboratory rats, yet it's found in our food. White sugar is denatured and causes mani-fold miseries, but the average American consumes 30 to 50 pounds a year. Denatured flour, rice and cereal continue to line supermarket shelves. Fruits and vegetables are coated with a petroleum product called paraffin wax to keep them fresh. No organ in the body is designed to handle it.

> *"If anyone defiles their temple, they will be destroyed .....which temple are you?" (I Corinthians 3:17)*

If a person is a meat eater, they must also be careful. Most commercially raised stock is injected with chemicals and hormones for various commercial reasons. The 11th chapter of Leviticus instructed the Hebrews as to what to eat and what to avoid in the animal, fish, and fowl kingdoms. The instructions follow a line of common sense. They were told to avoid vultures, ravens, pigs and eagles, as these are scavengers and eat putrefied, decaying bodies. The same holds true for aquatic creatures that live on the bottom and eat the garbage that settles there. In the East, pigs have been the sewer system for generations. The common sense advice is avoiding foods that would be harmful to the body.

While it's true that vitamins are a basic necessity to human survival, and front line helpers in so many bodily functions, most man made vitamins should be avoided. Words like enrichment and added nutrients should always be suspect. That usually means products have been laced with fillers or unnatural synthetics. A person need only walk down the cereal isle of a supermarket to see these.

In addition, most flour and rice are fortified with chemicals, as are bakery goods. It's high time they're exposed for the harm they do to mankind for profit. The FDA actually requires fortification by law! This is a tremendous multi-billion dollar profit center. Choose carefully your choice of commercial vitamins, as most are suspect. If a person is deficient in any area, there are plenty of vitamins available in natural God-given plants.

Natural vitamins are made of a combination of ingredients including enzymes and trace minerals, but taking one ingredient out of a plant, cooking it into oblivion, and then mixing it with fillers and other denatured products is self-defeating. Chemical companies take the natural plant and its wondrous inherent properties, and turn it into a synthetic drug. Artificial vitamins can cause many minor side effects, and in the long run, possible real damage. It has been proven that, though the chemical structures may be the same, synthetic and natural vitamins do not produce the same biological processes. Synthetics are most often useless for nutrition and harmful.

A good portion of vitamin brands are deficient and won't perform as advertised. Medical doctors generally don't recommend them, as there have not been enough studies completed to back up the outlandish claims that the vitamin companies make. The doctors are actually more familiar with drugs and dispense them freely. On the other hand, vitamin prescriptions are less than 1%. According to Sardi, author of *What's Best*, vitamin nutrients can cause a myriad of problems. For instance, vitamin B12 and riboflavin can cause cataracts or retinal damage in doses over 10 milligrams. Excess iron causes oxidation in the body. "All men essentially go into iron overload," Sardi says, "and men have twice the iron levels as women by the age of 40 and thus twice the disease rate, heart disease, cancer, diabetes and rates of infection." There are some positive effects catalogued in studies concerning multi-vitamins, but I say, "caveat emptor" or "let the buyer beware."

### *"DON'T BUY THE LIE"*

This vitamin business is another rattlesnake hole. Most so-called vitamin C's and B's and One a Day's, and other supplements are nothing more than synthesized chemicals, cooked, and adhered together with fillers and sweeteners. They have little or no value, and don't work properly, because they've been taken out of their natural form. If we consider water (H2O), and isolate the chemical properties, it's no longer water. In fact, the properties are totally different. Separated, they become explosive compositions and ingredients for things like the hydrogen bomb. An isolated part of a food, in most instances, isn't greater or more beneficial than the whole. Vitamin and drug companies, in the name of profit, have duped the public.

If a person does extended water fasts, deep healing energy will manifest to naturally clean and balance our bodily systems. Vitamins of all kinds should be avoided on elongated water fasts. The entire purpose of water fasting is to keep away from all nourishment and to rest the entire digestive, assimilation and elimination processes. Anything ingested that even slightly dampens autolysis from burning rubbish will take vital energy away from the deep, natural results of a fast. Any infringement from any nutritional source, no matter how minuscule, will minimize the process.

On juice fasts, however, a person can decide whether or not to add any healing herbs to the juices to assist in a particular problem. Since a person is already taking in nutrients and minerals, the focus of the juice fast is somewhat different. By all means, no matter which fast is chosen, a person should avoid synthesized, man-made vitamins. Aspirin, or any such so-called remedy, should also be totally avoided. It may alleviate pain, but the aspirin only covers symptoms and does absolutely nothing to heal or correct any problem whatsoever. Rather, it disrupts natural chemistry and can irritate organs. Everything affects the body and reacts in greater measure and with more sensitivity during a fast, so every type of medication is suspect.

The list of things to avoid grows daily. Most items are common sense. Alcohol is extremely harmful to our bodies and should be especially avoided during a fast. The liver works to eliminate poisons during a fast, but this function is completely blocked if alcohol is consumed. As the alcohol level rises, it spreads throughout the blood stream and affects other organs. It also seriously damages the heart, stomach and bowels. It has been proven that cells damaged by alcohol need much longer to recuperate.

Coffee, chocolate, heavy salted foods, pickled, moldy, charred, polyunsaturated, rancid, fried and smoked foods all contain certain levels of carcinogens. Meats are full of nitrate preservatives and other chemical to help animals grow and eat. A person should minimize exposure to pesticides, herbicides with dioxin, dyes, and colorings, and should avoid areas of oil refineries, chemical companies, paper mills, toxic waste dumps, power plants or any area with heavy industrial pollution. Household items right on your own shelves can be extremely dangerous like paint, strippers, cleaning products and lubricants. If they contain methylene chloride, throw them out immediately. Avoid pharmaceuticals, saccharin, PCB's, radiation, radon gas, and X-rays should be taken minimally.

Gum chewing should be avoided during a fast, as chewing will activate the saliva and enzyme process. Extreme hot and cold should also be avoided, unless one takes a steam bath or sauna, which is quite beneficial. During the fast all liquids should be of a moderate temperature to avoid any extreme reaction to an inactive system. Sexual activity should be eliminated during a serious fast, as the sexual organs shut down, and should be rested.

> *"Defraud ye not one another, except it be with consent for a time, that ye may give yourselves to fasting and prayer."( I Corinthians 7:5)*

There is much evil in the world designed to destroy us. Much of it is subtle, and often in places we least expect. We need to be wise in these things. *"The highway of the upright is to depart from evil; He who keeps his way preserves his soul." (Proverbs 16:17)*

# Part II
# Spiritual Fasting

>‹‹

After traveling the world for much of my life, studying and seeking God for a higher purpose, I finally chose to follow Jesus Christ as my spiritual master. Consequently, I draw inspiration, knowledge and wisdom from his words. Whatever your beliefs, the following chapters are meant to inspire you and to help you find abundant life. Wherever you find yourself or whatever your relationship with God, spiritual fasting will bring you closer to the purity and truth.

# Not If You Fast,
# but "When You Fast"

⇥⇤

> *"Moreover, when you fast, do not be like the hypocrites, with a sad countenance. For they disfigure their faces that they may appear to men that they are fasting. Assuredly, I say to you, they have their reward. But you, when you fast, anoint your head and wash your face, so that you do not appear to men to be fasting, but to your Father who is in the secret place; and your Father who is in secret will reward you openly." (Underline added) (Matthew 6:16-18)*

Jesus instructed His disciples on how to pray, give and fast. Jesus didn't say if you fast, if you pray, or if you give. He specifically said when you pray, when you give and when you fast. He didn't leave these activities open for debate. Praying, giving and fasting were activities He wanted His disciples to engage in. Jesus didn't present fasting as some radical program for fanatic zealots, or just for advanced holy men. He taught fasting as one of three basic premises for practical spirituality. Fasting is basic to the victorious life of a disciple of Jesus. Without fasting one won't and can't achieve the potential found in his teachings.

Jesus encourages his disciples to fast in order to overcome the many tribulations that afflict them. Jesus said, *"In the world you shall have tribulation, but be of good cheer, I have overcome the world." (John 16:33)* We too can overcome! Jesus advises that *"when you fast"* this is how you're to proceed. He counseled his disciples to fast discreetly, to wash their faces, and not to make a show of it. Fasting is not a matter of pride, rather it humbles a person. This next verse excites me!

> *"If you humble yourselves and seek my face, I will open the portals of heaven and pour out a blessing upon you so large that you cannot even receive it." (Malachi 3:10)*

You're saying that we should actually give up eating for periods of time? And, you say there's a reward and that I can do things I would not ordinarily do if I don't eat? Yes, but only if fasting is done properly. Fasting is designed to get the attention off ourselves and unto deeper spiritual things. Jesus says we should act as if all is normal. And then he says we should also pray. Jesus provides a supernatural key to gain extraordinary faith to accomplish things in life we could not normally do!

Fasting isn't a way to twist God's arm and make Him our order supplier. No, God has revealed the power of fasting and prayer as tools to help us accomplish things that are too difficult to do any other way. He did not present fasting as a means to accomplish great human feats, to bring attention to ourselves, and to become worldly heroes. The power generated from a fast comes from God through faith. No matter how long we fast, if it's not with the proper attitude, it may all be of non-affect spiritually. Isaiah speaks of a fasting that comes to non-effect.

> *"Why have we fasted they say, and you have not seen? Why have we afflicted our souls, and you take no notice?" (Isaiah 58:3)*

The Bible mentions fasting, and its synonyms supplication and mortification, seventy-five times. Proper fasting relieves burdens, begets wisdom and blessings, ignites revivals, gives direction, promotes healing, saves nations, expresses grief, gains protection, moves mountains and once started the greatest ministry of all time!

> *"Turn ye even to me with all your heart, and with fasting, and with weeping, and with mourning: And rend your heart, and not your garments, and turn unto the Lord your God: for he is gracious and merciful, slow to anger, and of great kindness." (Joel 2:12, 13)*

# Fasting and the Faith
# of a Mustard Seed

*"Now faith is the substance of things hoped for, the evidence of things not seen." (Hebrews 11:1)*

Faith is belief in a supernatural gift that's beyond our normal understanding. *"For by grace you are saved through faith; and that not of yourselves, it is the gift of God." (Romans 5:2)* Fasting and prayer build faith, and faith is necessary to do the exemplary. We're asked to have faith in the wisdom God has given us. *"Wisdom is health to the navel and marrow to the bones." (Proverbs 3:8)* Abundant life is within reach of everyone, but by faith we put into practice the knowledge to accomplish this end. *"Be doers of the word, not hearers only, thereby deceiving your own selves." (James 1:22)*

I've often asked myself, where's abundant life? How does one do the improbable? How do we overcome seemingly impenetrable and overwhelming obstacles? How do we obtain real and lasting healing from the ills that are so obviously around us all? How do we actually purify ourselves in mind, body, and soul? How do we harness such power? How does one reach one's potential?

*"He started to sing as he tackled the thing that couldn't be done, and he did it." Edgar A. Guest*

The disciples of Jesus once came to him frustrated and feeling very much the same way. They, too, had questions and felt utterly incapable and powerless against certain powerful demonic forces. Like many of us today, they were up against something that proved to be insurmountable, an immovable mountain. They were discouraged. They asked Jesus why they had not been able to cast a demon out of an epileptic man who had been uncontrollably falling into water and fires. Jesus immediately reprimanded them. He told them their inadequacy was simply the result of their unbelief. He told them they lacked faith. <u>He told them that such evil forces were only removed by prayer and fasting!</u>

Then Jesus said to them; *"....for assuredly, I say to you, if you have the faith as a mustard seed, you will say to this mountain, "move from here to there", <u>and nothing will be impossible to you."</u> (Matthew 17:20) (underline added)*

A mustard seed is miniscule, but faith the size of a tiny mustard seed holds unprecedented faith and power, and is a veritable spiritual key to an abundant life. According to Jesus, such faith leaves nothing to the impossible! He says we can have this spiritual key and experience levels of freedom in life not possible any other way.

*"I came to give you life, and to give it to you more abundantly." (John 10:10)*

Jesus tells us what's needed, what it takes and gives us a glimpse into the actual power of faith. He says there's a level of faith whereby nothing's impossible! He tells us of the awesome power of faith we've at out disposal. But how do we acquire such faith? Where is it? Where does it come from? A secular doctor may tell us we have an incurable disease, that there's no hope. Would we actually have no hope? Are we to believe the doctor and simply give up? But God says, "All things are possible to those that believe" (*Mark 10:27*) Jesus says we can move mountains with faith the size of a mustard seed and produce results normally unheard of, so do we believe the doctor in the natural who has limited abilities, or Jesus in the supernatural? Do we just accept the fact that we're helpless in such a desperate situation and give up? Do we put all our faith in the prowess of mankind? Is the doctor's vision the extent of possibility?

> *"Thus also faith by itself, if it does not have works, is dead." (James 2:17)*

How then does a person activate such faith? What key unlocks its power? By what process can we generate faith to do things seemingly impossible in the human realm? Curiously, Jesus said that this mustard seed, which is so tiny, grows to be the greatest of herbs. *"... which indeed is the least of all the seeds, but when it is grown it is greater than the herbs and becomes a tree, so that the birds of the air come and nest in its branches" (Matthew 13:32)*

That may be the reason he chose to use the mustard seed in his parable. Parables were made simple so everyone could understand, even a child. Jesus is simply trying to tell us what can become of a small amount of faith. Of course, most of us are familiar with the faith of the mustard seed, but it's the next verse that's indispensable and holds the key to success. It's this next verse that teaches us how to obtain the faith that'll move the mountain in our lives. It's this kind of faith that'll remove demonic forces in our lives we couldn't overcome in any other way.

> *"However, this kind does not go out, except by prayer and fasting" (Matthew 17:21) In (Mark 9:29) the same instruction is repeated: "So He said to them, this kind can come out by nothing, but prayer and fasting"*

The combination of prayer and fasting is the switch that turns on the supernatural depth of faith to handle overpowering demonic forces, whether they manifest physically, mentally, emotionally, or spiritually. Suddenly it's not so difficult to understand why doctors marvel at God's fasting principles in clinics after they've documented hundreds of thousands of fasts. Are we to ignore such a blessing? Once such knowledge is absorbed, do we continue to live mediocre lives? Do we choose to live beneath our privilege? Do we continue to languish with limited self-control? Do we continue to accept defeat and ill health? Do we make the investment? Now that we know that such faith is possible, do we PRAY and FAST?

How many of us wrestle daily with obstacles to abundant life such as health, bad attitude, and confidence, lack of energy, weight or damaged emotions. How often have we climbed in sight of the mountaintop only to be discouraged, only to weaken and slide back down? How many other things have we tried? Jesus has given us the key to overcome immovable mountains by a special faith, a depth of faith and power accessed by prayer and fasting.

It's written that the just walk by faith (*Habakkuk. 2:4*) Therefore faith is one of the main ingredients of life and should be used above all. Faith is called our shield. *"... above all, taking the shield of faith with which you will be able to quench all the fiery darts of the wicked one" (Ephesians 6:16)*

Where does faith come from? *"Faith comes by hearing and hearing by the word of God." (Romans 10:17)* With faith, we can attend to the dramatic, to the richness of life, to the very power of God. We need no longer be compromised or afraid of powerful impediments that bind us. Our faith is in direct proportion to the absence of fear in our lives. Where fear begins, faith ends. Where there's faith, there's no fear. Fasting and prayer activate faith, thus fasting and prayer destroy fear. We can't just quietly hold our faith. We must put faith into practice. In other words, we must pray and fast. Jesus taught faith is the key to miracles and healing. Throughout the Bible we read: *"Your faith has made you whole" (Matthew 9:22)"To your faith be it unto you." (Matthew 9:29)* And, what should happen if we just decide to forgo faith? What is the opposite of faith? The answer hits home, hard. *"......for whatever is not of faith is sin." (Romans 14:23)*

We might as well further divide the truth. If the opposite of faith is sin, then what do we get from sin? *"For the wages of sin is death" (Romans 6:23)* So fasting and prayer build the type of faith that removes sickness and death from our minds, bodies and soul. *"A wise man will hear, and increase learning; and a man of understanding shall attain unto wise counsel"( Proverbs 1:5)*

Jesus is love personified. Faith is given to us in love through Jesus. Faith is to be dispensed with love, lest we forget where it comes from. The principles and mysteries of prayer and fasting must also be taught in love and not forced upon anyone. *"And though I have the gift of prophecy, and understand all mysteries and knowledge, and though I have all faith, but have not love, I have nothing" (I Corinthians 13:2)*

# From Base Camp to the Mountaintop

**D**r. Albert Einstein said: *"Everyone who is seriously interested in the pursuit of science becomes convinced that a Spirit is manifest in the law of the Universe."* Of course, scripture tells us, *"The earth is the Lord's and all its fullness, the world and those who dwell therein." (Psalm 24:1)*

When we get serious and begin to approach truth with an extraordinary and heightened sensitivity, our adversaries will not yield territory readily. Therefore the battles can get particularly harsh. Do we want to take serious ground back from the enemy, whether spiritual, mental or biological? Then we must fast. And, shouldn't divine restoration techniques be superior to the often ineffective worldly platitudes and pervasive intellectual and remedial opinions? Those spiritually inclined might get some genuine consideration from the rest of us if they started to manifest "real" divine restoration power.

Whether they started with scripture, experience or science, it's curious how great spiritual leaders, scientists and physicians alike came to discover identical fasting principles. Like gravity, the benefits of fasting are inherent in nature and such truths have been discovered throughout the ages by those who sought them.

Dr. Bill Bright, founder of Campus Crusade for Christ, said

after his first 40-day fast: *"I had previously fasted, according to church rules and for religious reasons; but, never had I undertaken a scientifically designed program with supervision. Now I understand how and why to fast sensibly, for whatever reasons. My body lost 15 pounds permanently, and my mind and spirit gained immeasurably!"*

Fasting accomplishes two purposes. First, it reveals how much the flesh has taken control of our emotions. Fasting helps us face our addictions, compulsive behavior, depression and internal pain. Secondly, it serves in breaking the flesh's hold upon the will by drawing a distinguishable line in the sand. It's a magnifying glass that allows us to examine our conscious, as well as our unconscious patterns of living. Evil principalities have invested much towards controlling the subconscious patterns of mankind. Fasting exposes how much evil has subtly infiltrated our lives. (Evil is defined as anything, including the most subtle of effects that might harm us)

Do we really want to change the patterns that keep us in bondage, to live a life with meaning, driven by conviction, even willing to become the best we can be before God? Do we want to be empowered, to be able to free ourselves from objectionable subtle influences? Jesus' desire is for us to be significant, powerful, self-controlled and free from the most despicable and powerful of evil spirits. Do we want to get a grip on the subtle demons of fear, pride, hopelessness, worry, doubt and selfishness? They won't depart quietly, because their tentacles reach deep into our spirits, emotions and into our physical beings. Their presence will rise up against us with great force when we begin to fast before the Lord, but these patterns of wrongful living can be broken. Fasting can be an oasis of spiritual refreshment in a life that has become a desert of uselessness.

Fasting does not force God into action. If fasting becomes an empty ritual, it no longer has the power to affect the heart. God doesn't want nor does he need our works. He wants our hearts, and that's where the Israelites made their mistake! Their fasting insulted God. *"Do you really think that you can appease Me by offering your little fasts and expect Me to turn a blind eye to the corruption and rebellion in your heart? (Isaiah 58:2)*

The mode of fasting can come on spontaneously. For instance, when people grieve they sometimes automatically lose their appetites. Mourning and fasting are often mentioned together in the Bible. But does fasting move the hand of God? (*Isaiah 58:6*) indicates fasting isn't designed to move the hand of God, but to make evil turn loose those things that rightfully belongs to us, like health, vitality and a sound mind. However, we must press in and demand the enemy to release some things. The best way to press in and be proactive is to fast. Evil often controls territory in our lives and the lives of our loved ones. Fasting is a key that breaks loose the bonds of wickedness. Some people are so bound that only fasting and prayer can ultimately release them from powerful wicked chains of darkness like addictions, lust, hate or unforgiveness.

The very foundation of a spiritually successful fast is repentance. Unconfessed sin will hinder a fast. Here are several things we can do to prepare the heart: Confess every sin that God calls to our remembrance and accept his forgiveness (*1 John 1:9*) Seek forgiveness from all those we've offended and forgive all who have hurt us (*Mark 11:25; Luke 11:4; 17:3,4*) "...*present your bodies a living sacrifice, holy, acceptable to God...*" (*Rom. 12:1*)

Fasting does not change God; it changes us. We fast because we want God more than we want food. God won't respond to what we do, but to a change of heart, and it's here where we come to the deepest purpose of fasting. Sure, fasting brings immeasurable physical and mental benefits, and more, but ultimately fasting is a tool to help us change our hearts before God, to remove even the strongest of impediments. Fasting isn't something we offer God; rather it assists in offering ourselves to God.

Most of us would sacrifice much for someone we deeply love, but self doesn't like to go hungry. During a fast, self may raise its ugly head. There may be a wrestling match about who comes front and center, self or God. "*Then Jesus said to His disciples, "If anyone desires to come after me, let him deny himself and take up his cross, and follow me."* (*Mattew16:24*) Most of our tribulations stem from selfishness, from not letting God take control.

Though practiced by few, fasting is the greatest rejuvenating elixir known to man. It'll purify, heal, and restore us. So simple, yet still it's seldom understood. People continue to perish for lack of knowledge.

> *"The biggest problem facing the world today is not people dying in the streets of Calcutta, and not inflation, but spiritual deprivation . . . this feeling of emptiness associated with feeling separate from God, and from all our sisters and brothers on planet Earth."—Mother Teresa, 1979 Nobel Peace laureate*

Doctor Buchinger noted in *ABOUT FASTING: A ROYAL ROAD TO HEALING*, on page 10: *"During the five-thousand odd years of humankind's history which today we can survey, fasting represented, in all ages and climes, a way of healing and sanctification of far-reaching importance. The religious fast, which we find in all the higher religions of humankind, served at the same time to preserve the health of the body, the temple of the immortal soul. But, greatly to the loss of sick humanity, the healing fast was overlooked by medicine during the many decades of scientific-materialistic thought. Newly discovered at the turn of the 20th century, it has today regained a worthy position as a royal road of healing. . . .We must restore fasting to the place it once occupied in an ancient hierarchy of values 'above medicine'. We must rediscover it and restore it to honor, because it is a necessity."*

# The "Seek Ye First" Fast

✥

*"When you seek me with all your heart, I will be found by you" (Jeremiah 29:13, 14)*

When a person is willing to set aside the instinctual appetites of the body to concentrate wholly on God, they demonstrate to God they mean business, that they're seeking with all their heart. Fasting is an endeavor of wholeheartedness. The *Seek Ye First Fast* is purely spiritual in focus, not longer than ten days, and undertaken with water only. It can be longer, but such fasts should only be undertaken by a person with ample experience.

*"Yet even now, return to me with all your heart, with fasting. . ." (Joel 2:12).*

The *Seek Ye First Fast* is practiced to seek God's purpose for our lives. It's a complete break from any external nourishment, and undertaken to subjugate our thoughts and desires completely to the thoughts and desires of God. It should be undertaken with a spirit of genuine piety, with a spirit that neither despairs in adversity, nor is elated with pride. On the contrary, the firmer our confidence in divine fidelity, the more we'll practice humility and penitence. I believe Jesus undertook such a fast in the wilderness as he prepared for public ministry.

*"Pythagoras said that the most divine art was that of healing. And if the healing art is most divine, it must occupy itself with the soul as well as with the body; for no creature can be sound as long as the higher part in it is sickly." Apollonius of Tyana*

Scripture says, *"For My thoughts are not your thoughts, nor are your ways my ways, says the Lord. For as the heavens are higher than the earth, so are my ways higher than your ways, and my thoughts than your thoughts."(Isaiah 55:8)*The *Seek ye First Fast* is practiced *to* clean away all impediments that would get in the way and bog us down, like useless thoughts and feelings that clutter the heart. It burns through nonsense and corrosion on every level so that we can reunite our senses, minds, and hearts with our spiritual source. The *Seek ye First Fast* seeks to unite us with the ultimate healing and purifying source for the soul. It helps us to access the ways and thoughts of God.

*"But seek ye first the kingdom of God and His righteousness and all these things shall be added to you." (Matthew 6:33)*

Through fasting experiences, I've realized many benefits, like health, maintaining optimum weight, a good chemical balance and detoxification. I've strengthened my constitution, felt younger and sharpened the mind. As I continued to fast, I found myself seeking deeper meaning. If I sought God's kingdom before anything else, maybe I needn't be overly concerned with my own selfish desires. After all, God knows better than I do what I really need. He says he'd give me the desires of my heart if I trusted him. The *Seek Ye First Fast* has taken me to new levels of understanding and purpose in my life. It has helped me to put God first in my life, and I've realized so many of his blessings.

When we open our hearts and minds to God, we bulldoze our limited desires out of the way so he can operate. We're his children, and like any father, he wants to give us the best. What could be more uplifting and purifying than connecting with the ultimate energy and wisdom of God? What energy in the universe could supply more direction, balance and healing? When we focus all our attention on the God's energy, we commune with the same spiritual power Christ used to perform his miracles. We commune with the same power that created every cell in our bodies and on the earth. We commune with the energy that maintains creation, and with the very energy that created the scientists.

Solomon was considered the wisest human that ever lived. He gave us the Proverbs, which are practical patterns and knowledge for everyday life. When God told Solomon he could have anything he wanted, Solomon chose wisdom. He could have asked for riches or power, or anything else. God gave Solomon the wisdom he asked for, but because Solomon sought first God's wisdom, God also added tremendous other blessings onto him.

Job, a rich man, blessed with everything a man could desire in this world became the center of a dispute between God and Satan. Satan said that the only reason Job was so good and prospered was because God had a protective hedge around him. God said Job was a good man nonetheless, with or without the hedge. To prove His point, God removed his protective hedge. Satan attacked with a fury and Job ended up losing everything he had, his family, his vast wealth, and on top of it all, his body was sick and covered with boils. His neighbors saw Job's pathetic state and told him he should just curse God and die. But Job remained focused and faithful. He remained God-centered and never gave in. No matter his condition he continued to seek God. Eventually, God blessed Job and restored everything he lost, but this time a hundred fold! Seek ye first!

> *"When the body fasts the soul is hungry"*
> *Dr. Otto Buchinger*

The *Seek ye First Fast* opens our hearts and minds completely and unconditionally to God, It's the ultimate meditation, removing everything, even our most basic urge for food out of the way. It connects us directly with the absolute energy and purpose of God. It's an indefinable sacrifice of our mind, body, and soul to his purpose. Medical data not withstanding, spiritual fasting is neither the way of the medical establishment nor the rudiments of some man-made healing system. It's God's way, perfectly supernatural and free!

There are those that claim fasting to be foolish. But even scientists and doctors can't measure God in a test tube. They say we can't prove he's real. If we waited for proof on everything we do or say, we would severely limit ourselves. Some things are done on faith, and the faith to accomplish the extraordinary, as we've learned, is built by prayer and fasting. Fasting may sound like a foolish and simple thing to do, but the results are wondrous and undeniable. A spiritual fast is conducive to every facet of mind, body and soul. The *Seek ye First Fast* allows our beings to assimilate the God's divine energy into every part of our being. Even skeptical science has slowly begun to discover fasting and its mysterious benefits. But they have a long way to go in allowing God and his principles into the equation.

> *"But God has chosen the foolish things of the world*
> *to put to shame the wise, and God has chosen the*
> *weak things of the world to put to shame the things*
> *which are mighty." (I Corinthians 1:27)*

Fasting, along with prayer, is the quickest and most powerful way to remove any obstacle between ourselves and God. If we're serious about connecting with God, serious in finding his will for our lives, serious about detoxifying and healing, fasting is the ticket. God's pure energy is indispensable to the natural forces of water, air, earth, fire, mind and intellect. According to scripture, it's the energy from which all other energies and elements are made. If we seek this absolute energy, all the other energies will balance and fall into place. God's energy balances and regulates planets, suns, and stars.

When one plugs into God, it's like putting bacteria into the sun. Impurity will be destroyed. Similarly, when a person takes their mind, body, and soul to God, everything will be purified.

Dr. Paul Bragg relates: *"When you fast you are working with nature. God and nature will not perform a miracle until we're willing to bring our lives and habits into conformity with nature's laws."*

God created nature and its inherent laws. He's the lawgiver. God does not change. Nature does not change. It'll react to things we do. If our habits are bad and we poison ourselves, poison will do what it has to do and the body will react the way it has to.

Athenaeus, a Greek physician said long ago: *"Fasting cures diseases, dries up bodily humors, puts demons to flight, gets rid of impure thoughts, makes the mind clear, the heart purer, and the body sanctified, and raises man to the throne of God."*

When we begin the *Seek ye First Fast*, we're on the verge of a special realm of faith that's reserved only for those that pray and fast. It's a realm God says we can only achieve by prayer and fasting. It's a realm that moves mountains and removes the most stubborn of demonic forces. It's a realm where only he is first. I can only thank Him for this realization.

> *"If thine eye be single, your whole body will be full of light." (Matthew 6:22) (paraphrase)*

Material life and all its temporary trappings are like a lot of zeroes in our lives. If we concentrate on the zeroes, we never really get anywhere. But if we put the One in front of the zeroes, we become rich indeed. The One makes our zeroes valuable. If we seek God first, make Him number one in our lives, we'll access his glory and blessings.

> *"For what profit a man if he gains the whole world and loses his own soul?" (Mark 8:36)*

God has promised that if we follow his ways, he'll restore us. He has promised to add years to our lives. He has promised us abundant life. He has promised to restore the things in our lives that evil and sin have destroyed.

> *"So I will restore to you the years that the swarming locust has eaten..." (Joel 2:25)*

# Fasting with a
# Spiritual Formula

*"Thy words were found, and I did eat them; and thy word was unto me the joy and rejoicing of mine heart..." (Jeremiah 15:16)*

When the body fasts, the soul is also hungry. In order to fast and seek God, one needs sufficient peace and quiet, as well as a break from everyday routines. A deeper inner self may be felt for the first time. To support the process, spiritual food is necessary. Holistic healing is gaining popularity, as people realize their connection to God's natural laws, but complete healing involves more than just healing the physical and mental properties. True health reflects the relative balance between mind, body and spirit. There can't be a problem in one area without it reflecting in another. All healing comes from within, from the power of spirit. We must activate this healing power within.

*"...Physician, heal yourself." (Luke 4:23)*

Once there was a person who owned a birdcage. Its beauty and meticulous construction were known far and wide. Everyday this person polished the cage with utmost patience and dedication. They used the softest cloth made with special fabric, blends and weaves. The polish was the finest mixture of paste imported from faraway lands. Everyone that saw this cage admired it. The bars were uniform, made of gilded gold and silver. The door was on special bronzed hinges oiled to perfection. In the sun, the reflection of the cage was blinding. It was flawless. One day the bird died. This person is like so many of us, concerned with outward appearance, the body, hair, cloths, education, bank balance, sex, vacations and other worldly cares. A person can feed the body and mind with the best of everything on God's earth, but if they neglect the spirit within, the spirit will die. We're to be temples of the Holy Spirit.

> *"Or do you not know that your body is the temple of the Holy Spirit Who is in you, whom you have from God, and you are not your own? For you were bought with a price; therefore glorify God in your body and in your spirit which are God's." (I Corinthians 6:19-20)*

A spiritual fast is practiced to completely dedicate oneself to God and to eliminate every obstacle in the way. It can be of any length and done any number of ways. During a short spiritual fast, a person continues with most normal activities. A consecration fast is usually of extended duration and practiced with water only. A dedication fast is taking time to fast for a special purpose like intercession.

> *"Man does not live by bread alone, but by every Word that proceeds from the mouth of God." (Matthew 4:4)*

> *"...treasure the words of His mouth more than our necessary food." (Job 23:12)*

To compile this book, I've taken inspiration from worldwide research, history, great personalities, medical science, and personal experience and from scriptures. Though science is slowly adding credibility to fasting, it's still generally an idea that's considered somewhat mystical in nature. Though experience is one of our greatest teachers, fasting is still relegated to second-class status in the medical community. Spiritually, fasting is to be accepted and practiced by faith if we're to reach levels beyond the realm of science. In order to achieve results we must act on precepts and principles not always understood by man's intellect. Likewise, I don't understand all the deep hidden principles of fasting, but from experience, I do know they work.

> *"For My thoughts are not your thoughts, nor are your ways my ways, says the Lord. For as the heavens are higher than the earth, so are my ways higher than your ways, and my thoughts than your thoughts. So shall my word be that goes forth from my mouth; It shall not return to me void, but it shall accomplish what I please, and it shall prosper in the thing for which I sent it."(Isaiah 56:8, 9, 11)*

Love is stressed in scripture; in fact, it's the absolute and entire message. Jesus said to love God and your neighbor as yourself, were his greatest commands and the summation of his teachings. Would we want to live without love? We all know the benefits of love, how love feels, what love does for us, and for others. Because science can't tell us what love is, will we forego love until they figure it out? Do we forego fasting, because medical science would rather concentrate on things it can sell us? Love and fasting come from the same source and are given to us as gifts to live a more abundant life.

As I practiced the *Seek Ye First Fast*, innovative and exciting spiritual ideas flowed into my heart and mind. I began to string scriptures together and developed a process I call *"fasting with a spiritual formula"*. If a person has a goal in mind and wants to get from one place to another, they must see their way from one end to the other. If a person desires to pursue and accomplish the things of God, they must follow his plan. They must chart their course with his map.

*"Your word is a lamp to my feet, and a light to my path." (Psalms 119:105)*

Consider a person that wants to cross a stream without getting wet, and the only way across this stream is on stones exposed above water. An intelligent person would not just jump out onto one stone and then hope there were others nearby. A person with wisdom would find a place where there are enough stones to make it all the way across. When they find a place where stones are strung all the way across, they can make it easily. The key to the abundant life in scripture is available in much the same way. Jumping on one scripture and clinging to it will not get us to the goal. We need complimenting scriptures that will see us all the way to the goal.

*"For precept must be upon precept, percept upon precept, line upon line, line upon line, here a little, there a little." (Isaiah 28:10)*

There's a formula for all things found in scripture. Wisdom helps one rightly divide the Word and put the verses together. I began one fasting formula with the scripture. *"If you can believe, all things are possible to him who believes." (Mark 9:23)*

I was out on my first stone. I underscored the words *all things.* Does that mean what it says, all things? Were ALL things possible if I believed? Was I to believe like this? Did I believe? Then I put that scripture together with the exciting scripture about moving mountains and I had the beginning of spiritual formula.

*"So Jesus said to them, because of your unbelief, for assuredly, I say to you. If you have faith as a mustard seed, you say shall say unto this mountain, Move from here to there, and it will move and nothing will be impossible for you. However, this kind does not go out except by prayer and fasting." (Matthew 17:20-21)*

Here a little, there a little! When we put precept upon precept, we develop a solid formula for success in whatever we seek. We must use God's Word in formula for the words God spoke will never change. *"Heaven and earth shall pass away; my words will by no means pass away." (Matthew 24:35)* We don't build a house with just a foundation and live in it. No, we build walls, and put on a roof, and make doors and windows, and eventually we have a complete habitable home. The lines and precepts of scripture are spiritual laws. When we combine these laws and apply them in our lives, we put God's truth to work. The same God that created the body and bodily systems, and laws that govern nature, gave us scriptures to use for our edification and growth.

> *"As newborn babes, desire the pure milk of the word that you may grow thereby." (1Peter 2:2)*

The Bible contains over 3000 promises. God paid for them with His Son's very life. These promises are available to all. No one I know has 3000 problems.

Doctor Henry W. Vollmer wrote: *"Man's body was created according to the laws of physics and chemistry, which are the Creator's own laws. They never vary. His law is written upon every nerve, every muscle and faculty which has been entrusted to us. These laws govern cells, tissues and organs of the body as they carry on various functions. They operate largely through the complex network of nerves that run throughout the body. They act through the central nervous system, from which nerve impulses originate, and through the autonomic nervous system, that part of the network not under the direct control of the will."*

There's no limit to applying Biblical formulas. After a certain amount of success, I began to entertain greater projects and sought other formulas. I noticed things added to me. I broke habits, lost weight, regained vitality, attained to a more youthful zest, cleansed my entire being, And best of all, moved closer to God. I'm excited about the future and delving deeper into God's word and the potential that's available!

# Fasting and Prayer

*"So we fasted and besought our God for this, and He listened to our entreaty." (Ezra 8:23)*

*"And the prayer of faith will save the sick, and the Lord will raise him up..."(James 5:15)*

Fasting is a means of humbling ourselves before God, letting him know that we're willing to exchange and sacrifice physical comfort to seek his ways. As a spiritual discipline, fasting is the act of abstaining from feeding the body in order to focus fully on seeking God's face and feeding our soul. Fasting is a powerful discipline where God's Spirit can be accessed if we earnestly seek him. By fasting we can get the heart and mind right, obtain a personal awakening, overcome temptation, conquer moral impurity and discern God's will.

The combination is a most powerful discipline, and if we practice prayer and fasting, we'll be renewed and enjoy greater intimacy with God. Through fasting and prayer, our lives can be transformed on a grand scale. According to Scripture, when God's people fast with proper motives, seek his face with a repentant and contrite spirit, he hears from heaven and heals lives. Fasting and prayer can bring about revival on every level, change the direction of a nation, the nations of earth and fulfill the Great Commission.

The awesome power can be released through you through the enabling of the Spirit!

> *"If my people who are called by My name will humble themselves, and pray and seek My face, and turn from their wicked ways, then I will hear from heaven, and will forgive their sin and heal their land." (2 Chronicles 7:14)*

> *"For everyone that asks receives, and he who seeks finds and to him who knocks, it will be opened. Or what man is there among you, if his son asks for bread, will give him a stone? Or if he asks for a fish, will give him a serpent?" (Mat 7:8-10)*

> *"Therefore I say to you whatever things you ask when you pray, believe that you have them and you will receive them." (Mark 11:24)*

We need to be specific when we pray. A man named Albert was researching grizzly bears in the wilds of Alaska. He was a righteous man. One day a huge grizzly reared up on its hind legs in front of him. The bear stood over ten feet tall! Albert began to back up as he fought to regain his nerve. Unfortunately, his foot found a deep pit and he lost his balance and fell in. He knew this was the most serious situation he'd ever been in. The ferociousness and tremendous size of the bear that postured over him provided few options. Albert knelt to pray. A scripture he'd learned in Sunday school years ago ran through his head. *"...The effective fervent prayer of a righteous man avails much." (James 5:16)*

Albert firmly believed prayer was his passport to provision! The bear snarled and began to slowly slide down into the pit towards him. Albert prayed hard. "Lord, make this be a Christian bear." Albert's prayer was unlike any he'd ever prayed. "Lord, a Christian bear!" Every tiny cell in his quivering body flung open doors and each cell spouted a tiny prayer, and each minuscule prayer joined each other prayer, and together with Albert's soul at large combined feverishly in symphonic unison. Growling ferociously, the bear continued to inch towards Albert. Locked eyeball to eyeball, Albert cried out aloud. "Lord, please, Lord, I love you Lord. Please, Lord, hear my prayer. Lord, make this be a Christian bear." By this time the snarling bear had made its way to Albert's side. "Oh Lord, please. I beg you, please a Christian bear." Just then the bear knelt down next to Albert, folded his huge paws, and bowed his head. The last thing Albert heard was the bear praying, "Lord, bless my food."

God has linked prayer to fasting. They're inseparable and keys to deep supernatural communication and the greatest one-two punch available to us. Fasting magnifies the sincerity of prayer and adds urgency, intensity and focus. Prayer in turn magnifies the effects of a fast. One shouldn't fast without prayer. As we regard the benefits of prayer and add the principle of spiritual formula, we can only imagine what power the combination may have!

We find that prayer cleanses us from secret faults. *(Psalm 19:12-14)* It keeps evil from having dominion over us. Prayer has the power to hold us up so we don't slip and fall. Prayer keeps a person from the path of the destroyer. *(Psalm 17:4-5)* Prayer has the power to govern our tongues. *(Psalm 141:3)* Prayer has the power to open our eyes so that we can see clearly. *(Psalm 119:118)* Prayer brings forth the Holy Spirit and salvation. *(Acts 2:4, I John 5:16)* Prayer is the highest use to which speech can be put. The combination of prayer and fasting builds spiritual muscle. When a person fasts and prays, nothing is impossible!

> *"Is this not the fast I have chosen: to loose the bounds of wickedness, to undo the heavy burdens, to let the oppressed go free, and that you break every yoke?"( Isaiah 58:7)*

But if we fast without sincerity, we ultimately fast for non-effect. Just as in a physical fast, if we have a bad attitude, we'll not achieve prime results. God warned Jeremiah: *"When they fast, I will not hear their cry; and when they offer burnt offering and an oblation, I will not accept them..." (Jeremiah 14:12)*

During a fast we can pray for forgiveness, and in this process of repentance we'll be released from reaping anything we've sown. This is the best deal going in spirituality. It's the reason Jesus died for mankind, to relieve us from the blemishes of our sins and to bring us salvation.

> *"If we confess our sins, He is faithful and just to forgive us our sins, and to cleanse us from all unrighteousness." (I John 1:9)*

# Miracles and Healing

As language evolved, the word health developed from the word hal, which initially meant holy, whole, and health simultaneously. There was no distinction and the words were interchangeable. Today we speak separately in terms of health and whole. In recent years there's been a move back to integration of whole and health with the term "holistic health".

God is in the healing business spiritually, emotionally and physically. Jesus healed everywhere he went. He even healed when he wasn't aware, like the woman who reached out and touched his garment and was automatically healed. Years of pain and suffering can be dissipated by the force of God's healing power. People often turn to God to beg for healing when healing is right in front of them. With the advances of surgery and drugs, our society has become impatient and expects things to happen immediately. But healing is natural, a spiritual birthright, and under the proper conditions will happen in most cases. But healing can take time. In some cases it can take a year or more to heal. What took years took break down can take time to build up. We must be patient.

> *"But let patience have its perfect work, that you may*
> *be perfect and complete, lacking nothing."*
>
> *(James 1:4)*

A healing fast is like any other fast, but it brings with it special considerations. We've already explored the fact that fasting unlocks normally inaccessible possibilities. With this in mind, we can be confident and have faith in the fact that even a difficult healing is possible during a fast. Healing is repair, and repair requires care and rest. If a person breaks a leg, they must stay off the leg until the bone sufficiently heals before they can walk again. When there's a serious problem or sickness, a person needs to use the same common sense. A healthy person does not need bed rest when they fast, but can maintain a normal, albeit moderate schedule. Again, this takes common sense. But if a person is under serious repair, they should rest as much as possible. Any heavy physical activity should be eliminated during most fasts, but altogether during an elongated fast when specific healing is the focus.

A person should be prepared to allow for the effects of healing. During a healing fast, things often get worse before they get better. While the body is engaged in the elimination of poisons and other unwanted debris that caused the sickness, a person may experience aches and pains and other discomforting symptoms. The body may focus energy almost exclusively on the problem area, thereby ignoring or down sizing other functions and causing additional discomfort.

*".... your health shall spring forth speedily."*
*(Isaiah 58:8)*

The empirical explanation of what happens during healing is that many functions of the organs are greatly reduced, so power inherent in the body is diverted and able to concentrate its power on the damaged or poisoned areas.

*"....the prayer of faith will heal the sick....pray for*
*one another that you may be healed."*
*(James 5:15, 16)*

Should we wait for a miracle or for healing to fall out of the sky? There are things we can do to bolster faith. We can move mountains by prayer and fasting. A seed bears fruit of its own kind.

*"But be doers of the word, not hearers only, deceiv-
ing yourselves." (James 1:22)*

Healing and miracles are often confused. People pray for healing, and when nothing happens right away, they're discouraged,
believing they've received nothing. It should be noted that an
instantaneous healing is called a miracle. A miracle is different than
healing. Healing takes time. A miracle happens instantly and defies
reason. If you cut your finger, and it immediately healed, that would
be a miracle. But healing does not work like that. The finger will
heal naturally, day by day as nature intended. Many people receive
a healing and aren't even aware of it, because they don't understand
the process. The person must be patient and let healing happen.

We may pray for a miracle, but God may give us a healing
instead. Many times, as I've discovered in my own life, God won't
provide the miracle I seek, because I can learn so much more by
going through a healing. I've come to realize this after I once
prayed for a miracle and expected to arise from my affliction immediately. I prayed and prayed and nothing happened. Actually, something did happen, but it wasn't what I'd had in mind. Then I became
a bit more sensitive to what was happening. I became patient, which
is exactly what I needed as much as the healing. I healed for quite
some time and realized and learned many wonderful things during
this time. I also realized that if God had given me a miracle, I may
have missed all the wisdom and knowledge I gained doing it his
way. We must be sensitive to where God leads. If we stubbornly
cling to the idea of a miracle, when he offers healing, we may miss
the healing and the wisdom that accompanies it.

*"Let patience have its perfect work, that you may be
complete, lacking nothing." (James 1:4)*

Healing is natural and under God's ultimate control. A miracle
on the other hand is a special boon from God. It's divine intervention. Doctors have found malignant tumors or incurable disease and

inform the patient they have such and such time to live. When the calamity disappears due to a miracle the doctors have no answers. From my experience, though fasting is a process and may take, I've come to view fasting as God's miracle.

# Self Control

*"Like a city whose wall are broken down, is a man
who lacks self control." (Proverbs 25:28)*

Fasting bestows upon the sincere practitioners access to the very
building blocks of abundant life, such as mental clarity, spiritual depth, physical health, and a fundamental fruit of the spirit,
self-control. *(Galatians 5:22, 23)*

And how do we recognize those that truly lead spiritual lives?
Jesus said, *"You'll know them by their fruits" (Matthew 7:16)* One
of the most imperative fruits to achieve in our lives is self-control. If
we have no self-control we can't cope in today's world of temptation. Our society is geared towards sex, power, excess and greed.
But Jesus says: *"Be of good cheer...I have overcome the world."*
*(Mark 6:50)* This verse does not mean we're to give up things of the
body. Quite the contrary! When we add the spiritual dynamic to our
lives, to our flesh, we enter a dimension where all the things we
strive for can be accomplished properly, not according to the
worldly ways, but according to God's ways.

*"Heaven and earth shall pass away, but my words
shall never pass away." (Matthew 24:35)*

Fasting is the benchmark of self-control. As we know, food is the greatest appetite. Lust is natural desire out of control, whether concerning food, drink, sex, anger, or greed. We all have natural desires, and when pursued according to spiritual principles, they can be totally fulfilled and satisfied.

> *"But I keep my body, and bring it into subjection, lest that by any means, when I have preached to others I myself should be a castaway."*
> *(I Corinthians 9:27)*

> *"For if you live after the flesh, you will die; but if you through the Spirit do mortify the deeds of the body, you will live." (Romans 8:13)*

# My Personal Fasting Schedule

*"Know Thyself" Socrates*

As I became more aware of the extraordinary benefits of fasting, I tried different types of fasts before settling on a program that works best for me. We all have different bodily chemistry, metabolism, constitutions, genetics and different reasons to fast. And, each of us has a distinct relationship and walk directed by God.

I do both water and juice fasts in no particular order. I also do grape fasts. I simply pick one or the other according to how I feel at the time. A juice fast is obviously easier, as there's some nourishment. I buy concentrate from the health food storeWhen I fast for purely spiritual reasons, I usually do a water fast. I like to seek God's will for my life without allowing any intervention. I strive to allow the deep fire of God to have its way in my spirit, mind and body.

I borrowed my fasting schedule and procedures from a few sources and experience. I had to change a few habits, for fasting will have no lasting benefits if a person continues bad habits. I incorporate my fasting with a total health program, physically, mentally and spiritually. It's contradictory to pray to the Lord for a physical healing and well-being and continue with bad habits, overeat and consume unwholesome foods.

*"Therefore to him who knows to do good and does not do it, to him it is sin." (James 4:17)*

I've learned to fast to find the Lord's will in my life. I've leaned that I'll invariably reap what I sow from my lifestyle, so I try and eat only foods and herbs God created. I avoid addictions, rest properly and exercise every day. I've also read God's word, for there's still so much too learn and room for growth, so I feed my spirit daily.

I've tried various lengths of fasts, and finally settled on a consistent program fasting 1 day a week, every week. One day a week totals 52 fast days a year! My last meal is the evening before, and my next meal is the morning after, which in essence is a 36 hour fast. For a good part of this period I'm asleep. Those extra few hours at rest are very beneficial. There's no activity I can't perform while practicing this one day a week fast. I try to do the same day every week to keep a rhythm, unless something really special comes up. Then I fast on the previous or succeeding day.

I find my energy level has improved, my mind has sharpened, my strength has increased, my digestion is better, my immune system is strong, my skin tone is smoother, my elimination is more regular, and my weight stays near its optimum. Fasting has helped me get closer to God and realize more of my potential!

Every season, spring, summer, fall and winter, I fast 7-10 days. If I feel the need for detoxification, deep healing therapy, or if I have a deep, spiritual need, I may even extend the fast. On the average I fast about seventy-five days a year, or approximately 25% of the year.

Most often, my fast is easy, with days of extreme clarity and feelings of well-being, and there are also days that seem as if I'm walking through a fire, but the fast never fails to produce extraordinary results. When the fast is most difficult, it's doing its deepest and best work. I've found fasting creates the most ideal conditions for personal growth and healing.

I'd thought I was pretty healthy after being on my program for over a year, but as I continued to fast and develop, I began to find new areas that I didn't know existed. I learned there are no limits to where a person can go and how healthy a person can be. *"All things are possible to those that believe." (Matthew 19:26)* Early on in my fasting endeavors, I awoke one day and noticed how smooth and lubricated my joints were. I walked around all day, moving my fingers, arms and legs enjoying my newfound youthful fluidity. I've come to understand well the scripture: *"But he, who heard and did nothing, is like a man that built a house upon the earth without a foundation, against which the stream beat vehemently, and immediately it fell. And the ruin of that house was great." (Luke 6:49)*

I also learned there's no searching God's ways, that no matter how deep I go, there is always more. I often find myself marveling at what's happening to my entire being. I feel youthful, restored, clear, and a spiritual fire I can't get enough of. As my fasting continues, and as I grow and learn, I'm astonished at the energy I access. Every fast I undertake unlocks a new dimension, a new facet, and a more robust nature. I marvel at God's principle and I'm so happy I found his truths. It's true, God gives us abundant life! Thank you Lord for the freedom song in my heart!

# Bibliography

*"In a multitude of counselors there is safety."*
*(Proverbs 11:14)*

It's impossible to list all the sources that have influenced this book. I began researching fasting and natural healing when I was seventeen. Let's say I'm more than three times that age now. The knowledge I've gained has come from a variety of sources, many continents, education and experience. Over the years, I've gone down many seemingly alluring paths that turned out to be no more than dead ends and empty promises, mere illusions, until I found Jesus Christ. I want to especially thank him for his sacrifice and love. I also want to thank all those who helped me along the way, the names of which are too numerous to mention.

**May God bless you, your endeavors and may you live in His abundance!**

"The Bible" (Unless otherwise noted all quotes are taken from the New or Old King James Versions)
"The Miracle of Fasting" Paul C. Bragg M.D. PhD
"Juice Fasting" Paavo Airola PhD
"Are You Confused?" Paavo Airola Ph.D.
"How to Get Well" Paavo Airola PhD

"Hypoglycemia" Paavo Airola PhD
"Fast Your Way to Health" Lee Bueno
"Fasting Can Save Your Life" Herbert M. Shelton
"Fasting: The Ultimate Diet" Allan Cott M.D.
"Fasting, a Way of Life" Allan Cott M.D.
"Fresh Vegetable and Fruit Juices" N.W. Walker D.Sc.
"The Essenes Gospels of Peace" International Biogenic Society,
    U.S.A. 1981
"Raw Food and Juices" Bircher-Benner
"Raw Fruits and Vegetables Book" Bircher-Benner
"Doctor Patient Handbook" Bernard Jensen D.C., Nutritionist
"Raw Vegetable Juices" Walker N.W., D.S.
"Field Guide to Medicinal Plants" Steven Foster, James A. Duke
    PhD
"The Herb Gardener's Mail Order Source Book" Elayne Moos
"North Winds Farm Directory" Paulo Oliver
"The Healing Herbs" Michael Castleman
"Culpepper's Complete Herbal and English Physician" Nicholas
    Cullpepper
"The Encyclopedia of Herbs and Herbalism" Malcolm Stuart
"Light, Medicine of the Future" Jacob Lieberman, O.D. Ph.D.

# www.jobasic.com

- **To order** additional books or to purchase quality herbs, reputable holistic products, along with numerous other *JoBasic* products and services, shop online at the *JoBasic* website of your choice. A percentage of each sale will go to your favorite charity or organization. Find a list of organizations at www.jobasic.com

- Order "Prevent Life Decay" by phone 1-866-BOOK (2665)

- **Important Note:** *JoBasic* provides free websites to charities, fundraisers, booster clubs, buying clubs, religious and other organizations. A percentage of the profit of each sale is electronically calculated and sent to the organization of your choice.

- **Books by Marvin Yakos**: "*Jesus vs. Jihad* "can be purchased at www.JoBasic.com or at your favorite bookstore or at most electronic bookstores.

Printed in the United States
57828LVS00005B/160-198

9 781591 606116